THE EXTENDED WAR DIARY OF A GERMAN POW

HELGA MCKEE

Published in the United States of America

Brilliant Books Literary
137 Forest Park Lane Thomasville
North Carolina 27360 USA

ISBN:
Paperback: 979-8-88945-483-0
Ebook: 979-8-88945-484-7

THE
EXTENDED WAR DIARY
OF A GERMAN POW

The story of a little German girl, as she remembers her experiences in war torn Germany, the endless days and nights, filled with fear, hunger, and the struggle to survive during World War II.

At the end of the war, Helga tells of her first encounter with American soldiers and how their kindness and generosity touched her in a way that led to an inner desire to someday live in this great country that everyone was talking about.: This" "America.". This "great USA."

It is an interesting and adventurous journey that takes place in three countries and tells of a child's life that would be quite difficult for many to envision today.

ACKNOWLEDGEMENTS

First and foremost, I would like to thank my 'Dad', Hans Gussmann, who encouraged me from the very beginning to write this book. I want to express my gratitude to my son Gary who has helped me edit my script. I would also like to thank several of my closest friends for their support and encouragement, especially Melanie Hughen. Much appreciation goes to my husband, Willie, for allowing me the time to write whenever I wished. Thank you for your love and patience, and to my children and grandchildren. Most of all, I would like to extend my utmost gratitude and many thanks to my son, Gary, who has supported and encouraged me throughout this entire project. He took my dad's place after he passed away and became my advisor and my critic, but most importantly, my 'Rock'. I thank you, Gary, from the bottom of my heart. I don't know what I would have done without you. Thank you for always being there for me, for your time, and for all that you gave of yourself. I am so grateful, and I love you.

CHAPTER I

BOMBS OVER NUREMBERG

I just walked in the house, sitting down my two bags full of groceries on the kitchen countertop; I decide to flip on the television before starting to put things away. CNN has a continuing coverage of the "Katrina Disaster" – what a catastrophe. My heart goes out to all the victims ripped from their homes with no place to go. Most lost all their belongings; many lost more than material things; human lives that cannot be replaced. I watch and stand still as a helicopter flies over a roof on which people seem to be stranded. One man is holding up a sign that reads, "Help us please."

Most of all the beautiful city of New Orleans is overflowing from raging floods. My husband and I had visited the city a couple of times before. I could not imagine that all of this had been destroyed. The rescue squads, police and firemen as well as the National Guard are all working fiercely to save lives and bringing everyone to safety. The entire Gulf Coast is suffering pretty much for this disaster.

I have now put my groceries away and poured myself a cup of coffee. I need to sit down for a minute to catch my breath. I think about 9/11; the horrible disaster that turned out to be; oh dear God, what is happening to our beautiful country? It seems as though one disaster strikes after another. My heart then prays silently for all the victims and the loved ones they have lost. Please God, give them all shelter and safety, reuniting them with their families and put their lives back to normal.

While pouring myself a second cup of coffee, my mind goes back to a long time ago, long before I ever came to this beautiful country that we call "America" or the USA! I was a little girl then, born at the beginning of World War II. I remember lots of things, especially in later years. Other incidents were told to me by my mother and other family members. We lived each day and night in fear for our lives.

It was another cold February night in 1943 and the noise of loud sirens shrieking through the night alerting all the citizens of Nuremberg to head for the shelters and take cover. As the British Royal Air Force was conducting one of its nightly air raids over the city, my Mother lifted me gently from my warm bed. She wrapped a blanket around me and pulled it over my head covering my ears to help drown out the noise of the loud and shrill sounding sirens. I wasn't quite four years old then and sort of a dainty little girl; therefore she carried me. She always tried her best to keep from waking me up and keep me from being afraid, but that was almost impossible due to all the loud noises. She always kept a large carry-on shoulder bag ready consisting of clothing, medicine, first aid items along with snacks and a small cuddly teddy bear that was my sleep mate. Carrying me and a shoulder bag on the other arm, she hurried out pulling the door shut and headed out to the street making her way alongside other people to the neighborhood fallout shelter. Everyone was in a hurry to get inside. Some of the people tried to bring as much luggage as they could carry, trying to bring all of their prized possessions for no one knew for sure what they would find once the air raid was over, nor what, if anything, they would have left. It was pitch dark outside; the city was under a strict law that demanded total blackout during the night. No light was to be seen from any windows, doors or other exposed openings reflecting light to the outside. Anyone not obeying these rules faced a strict fine and the possibility of some jail time. Each person was allowed to carry a small dim-lit flashlight on the way to the shelter, but if the sound of a plane was heard, it had to be extinct immediately.

The shelter would fill quickly with worried and anxious people. The interior of the shelter was lit by dim lights; one area consisting of bunk beds, cots, tables and folding chairs. Then there was a storage room that contained non-perishable foods and water, with another room stocked with oxygen tanks, medical supplies and first aid items. I looked around at all of the worried-looking faces. No one said much of anything. My mother laid me down on one of the cots and sat down beside me. She tried her best to keep me calm and said, "Go back to sleep," but there were so many people and lots of children of all ages. Some of the little ones were crying. We were all told to keep as calm and quiet as possible, mainly being that it caused the declination of the oxygen. Everyone waited and listened to the sound of nearing planes as they became more intense. The same questions ran through everyone's mind: Where would they drop the bombs tonight and what was awaiting us after the air raid was over. Would we have a home to go back to and a nice warm bed to slip into? My mother looked so worried. I could see it in her eyes. She was only 22 years old then, but she had a big responsibility resting on her young shoulders. She had to take care of me while my Dad was away at war and very seldom was permitted to leave to come home for a few days, part of Dad's furlough.

My Dad fought in foreign countries all over the Balkans, Poland, Russia and France; this was a duty that he and every other soldier had to perform. He was wounded twice and spent some time in a military hospital from leg, arm and hand wounds. War was an ugly and fearful experience. It was not like it used to be; the happiness, peace of mind and contentment seemed to have left all German people with life becoming such a struggle. There was the constant day to day and night to night fear of losing our lives. It wasn't always this bad. From the beginning of the war in 1939, most all battles were fought in foreign countries, but now Germany was getting paid back. We began to feel the big fear of the unknown that was headed towards us with many innocent elderly men, women and children losing their lives. We would all have to pay the price for Hitler's unjust actions. In January 1943, Germany lost 300,000 soldiers in Stalingrad, Russia with this startling event changing the lives of all Germans. Hitler began to dictate new orders and restrictions that affected everyone. It was to become the Total War with the logo being "Victory or Death."

Young boys were being drafted at the age of fifteen and men up to the age of fifty years old. Women were drafted to perform duties previously performed by men, which meant taking on factory jobs and all sorts of other duties. My mother, too, was called upon to perform her duty delivering telegrams for the Postal Service which she did riding a bicycle. While she rendered her duty to the "Fatherland", I was being kept by my paternal great grandparents. They lived in one of the many apartment buildings that were five stories high. The apartment that my great grandparents Meyer occupied was on the second floor, and, of course, those apartment buildings did not have any elevator, only lots of steps and staircases. The kids loved sliding down the railings including this kid, but I got fussed at for doing so. My mother's family also lived on the same street a few buildings down from the Meyers. In those days, there were individual stores on each street, a bakery where one would shop each morning for fresh baked "brotchen" (yeast hard rolls). There was also a dairy store for milk, butter, cheese and yogurt that, too, was purchased fresh each day. Also, there was a butcher shop and a small grocery store. People did not have refrigerators in those days, but we didn't need them because we bought our food fresh each day.

I can't remember seeing any canned foods in those days except for fruits and vegetables that people canned in jars for wintertime. I believe that people were much healthier back then consuming freshly cooked foods each day without having all the preservatives added that are now in our daily foods. I remember so well going shopping with Grandma Meyer. She carried all her goods in shopping nets and bags that were used over and over for this purpose. We had to walk several flights of steps and I always helped her, carrying one of her nets or bags. They had a wooden corner bench in the kitchen and I used to sit back there curled up and watch Grandma Meyer prepare all her delicious foods. She was a wonderful cook.

My great grandpa used to sit in his easy chair smoking his pipe and reading the daily Nuremberg paper; of course, there was no television in those days. Our news came from radio, newspaper or the weekly news at the local movie theater where the news was always shown before the main event.

I was an only child; no siblings. I always wished for a little brother or sister but Mom would tell me that because my Dad was gone so much they could never get together to order one, so I stayed an only child. I guess in a way it was good for my Mom's sake. She would really have had her hands full taking care of more than one and having to get up sometimes two and three times and head for the shelter. I look at my Mom again; gosh, she is so beautiful. She would turn heads wherever she went. Some people said she looked like a movie star. She had the blonde natural wavy hair, shoulder length, those sparkling blue eyes and high cheek bones, beautiful white teeth and a gorgeous figure. She could have been a model.

Mom was the second oldest of four girls. She also had an older brother Sam who fought and was wounded in Russia. He sustained a gunshot wound to his abdomen and upper thigh. He had to be left in a makeshift hospital as the German Army had to retreat for the Russians were invading that territory. They had to leave all their heavily wounded behind so no one has heard anything since 1944. We don't know if the Russians killed them all or captured and kept them as prisoners. The Red Cross tried several times to locate him and the other wounded soldiers, but without success. Then there was a younger brother named Hansl. He was next to the youngest sister Greta. The oldest sister was Erna and the younger sister next to Mom was Anna Lisa who would later marry an American Soldier and come to the USA.

My Mom's name was Elli. Mom's family really had a hard time in those days. They were poor and food was very scarce in their family. My maternal grandfather fought in World War I; he became heavily wounded and got a medical discharge. It was hard for him to find work and feed his family of eight. There was a layoff and he was among the ones to go. There were times when the older children actually had to go out and beg for food and money so the younger ones could eat.

My Dad came from a smaller family. He only had one younger brother who was four years his junior by the name of Robert. My Dad's name was Hans. When I was born my Mom was eighteen and my Dad was twenty years old. He was then called to the military before I was born and only got a few days leave of absence for the birth of his daughter after I was several days old.

My mother's voice calls me back to reality as she lifts me up from the cot where she had laid me down, "Come on Angel, it's time to go home" she said, the raid is over. We got our things together and got in line to head for the shelter's exit. The thought crosses my mind thinking what it would have been like if I had to get my own babies up in the middle of the night and head to a bomb shelter. I shudder at the thought.

None of us knew what was awaiting us outside of the shelter. Somehow everyone is hesitant and fearful to step outside, but we were lucky once more. The bombing took place in the Northern outskirts of Nuremberg. Thank God, we have a warm and cozy bed to go back home to. Ever since my Dad had gotten drafted in 1939, I got to sleep with my Mom in her large bed, but, of course, when my Dad came home on leave, which was very seldom, I had to sleep in my own room.

We lived in a nice middle class apartment building. Our apartment was on the second floor. It consisted of a small kitchen, a large dining/living room, two bedrooms and a bathroom. Our furniture was real nice in modern style. My bedroom was pink and white with all sorts of toys and a closet full of beautiful clothes. My Dad used to bring me clothes from foreign countries. For example, I remember the beautiful white rabbit fur coat with silver lining with a matching muff and cap that came from Paris, France. I had handmade shoes with beautiful carvings and colored insets from Turkey, handmade and embroidered dresses from Yugoslavia and Hungary. My parents also had a beautiful large doll house made for me with all of the furniture in it being hand carved of wood and beautifully decorated painting. Then, there was the collection of all my dolls. The then famous and popular turtle shell dolls; some of which were dressed in our traditional Tyrolean costumes.

We are back at the apartment and now going back to bed for a few hours. Mom had to get up pretty early so she could take me to my great grandparents' house before going to her telegram delivery job. Some mornings when she didn't have time to take me, she would put me on the street car and tell the conductor where to let me off. My grandmother Meyer usually held a look out from her window and if she saw me getting off the streetcar alone, she would hurry downstairs and meet me up at the street about one block away.

After getting the "good morning" hug from her, we would head back to the apartment to see Grandpa Meyer who also watched out the window puffing on his pipe. I always loved ringing the door bell and so I looked for that "Willy and Klara Meyer" name and pushed down on that button. I'd look up at Grandpa and he would give me that "come on up" motion with his arm. What sweet two people they were. It pains my heart when I think of the horrible way these two had to die, but more about this later.

When we got upstairs, I hugged Grandpa Meyer and sat down with him in the wooden corner bench behind the kitchen table. He would sit there with me and tell stories while Grandma was fixing our breakfast on the big wood stove. They burned coal in it too; it was the coziest place to me and I loved spending my days there. They would tell me about the times when my Dad and his brother were little boys and they used to watch after them while my grandparents were at work. Then, they would tell me all about the times when they got in trouble. Grandma Meyer never missed a day going to church. She was there at 7:00 each morning celebrating Mass and receiving Holy Communion.

One day, I, too, got in trouble. My Great Grandma would take me to the park down the street, and she sat on the bench with other friends that she knew who also kept their grand or great grandchildren. As we played and they talked, there was a beautiful water fountain with statues that held jugs and vases, so common in Europe, where water came pouring out. The weather was sunny but cool. It was one of those brisk March days. The water was splashing and so inviting into the bases of the fountain that my little friend Erika and I decided to go for a little swim in the fountain with clothes, shoes, socks and all of us emerged in that cold water. I can still remember that horrible chill and how cold that wind was blowing against our wet little bodies. Our teeth started to chatter as the two Grandmas came running toward us throwing their hands up in mid air with one shouting "Helga" and the other one "Erika." They were both fussing at us, taking us by the hand and heading down the street towards our apartment building.

Grandma Meyer took all my clothes off and sat me in a tub of warm water. After bathing and drying me off, she put dry clothes on me and made me sit in the corner on the wooden bench with a blanket wrapped around me. She washed out my wet clothes and hung them upon a string that was strung across the top of the stove. She sat my shoes on top of a wooden shelf so that all would dry before my Mom came to pick me up.

Unfortunately, on that particular day, my Mom came earlier than usual. As a matter of fact, I was still wrapped up in the blanket sipping my hot chocolate when she walked in. I thought "UH OH", and as I had anticipated, she started to ask all sorts of questions, why were my clothes all wet and hanging up, and why were my shoes wet, and why was I all wrapped up in a blanket." Well, my sweet old Grandma answered all the questions, but in a way so I wouldn't get in trouble. Her reply was something like, she thought I had lost my balance and fell in the fountain. I don't think that Mom bought it. She knew me and she knew how I loved getting into water and my passion for swimming, so I got fussed at on the way home

On another day, my Great Grandma told me that I could go to the neighborhood beauty shop to have my hair washed and styled while she shopped for groceries. The people that ran the shop knew me well and all of my family. I told the lady to fix my hair in a stylish updo like the movie stars were wearing. I also told her that my Grandma would pay for it when she picked me up. So, they fixed my blond natural curly hair into a fancy upswept hairdo like Betty Grable, Lana Turner and other film divas were wearing in the 40s.

It was Friday afternoon and my grandmother, who also worked, got off early and came over to meet up with me and Grandma Meyer which was her Mom. When they both walked into the beauty shop, they hardly recognized me. Then they smiled and chuckled a good laugh along with everyone else in the shop. After paying for my new hairdo, she and Grandma took me by the hand and walked down the street with me showing me off to everyone we knew. Everybody knew everybody on that street, so people were giving all sorts of compliments telling me how I looked like a little "movie star." Of course, I liked that! I loved going over to my paternal Grandmother's house whenever she was at home and could keep me. She let me get dressed up in her clothes, hats, shoes, etc. I even got to wear her jewelry and lipstick. I loved playing dress up, especially in grown up clothing.

CHAPTER II

DEEPER INTO WAR

As time went on, we grew deeper and deeper into war. My Dad was stationed in Bamberg and most weekends whenever possible, Mom and I would catch a train out of Nuremberg and go to visit him for the weekend. How I always looked forward to those visits as I did not get to see my Dad very much at all. My Dad was a supervisor over two-hundred women that worked in a plant making bombs and ammunitions and since he was a demolition expert and had been schooled in Berlin, he had been appointed to this position; of course, it was all military operated.

He also played music in the military band and they had music on Friday and Saturday nights. I got to go and watch my Dad play the drums and hear him sing. He would then call me up and let me sing a song over the microphone. Of course, that made my night and I received big applause from the audience.

Finally at 8:30, my Mom would take me over to the housing barracks and a baby sitter took over the care until Mom and Dad came back.

On Sunday morning, we attended Mass at a Catholic Church. Then, we ate lunch at a nearby restaurant before Mom and I headed back to Nuremberg. It was always so sad, having to say good bye to Dad. When we got back, we had to unpack and get ready for the upcoming Monday and the work week ahead.

One afternoon when Mom came to pick me up from Grandma and Grandpa Meyer's, she had been crying. She had seen her Mom that afternoon and was told that she had been diagnosed with incurable breast cancer. She had waited too long before she went to see about herself. In those days they did not have all of the medications that we have nowadays, and she didn't have much time left. She died at the young age of forty-five leaving twelve-year-old and fifteen-year old girls and an eighteen-year old son behind. They all still lived at home.

Mom's oldest sister, Erna, stayed there and took care of them; her husband was away at the front. She also had a little girl of her own "Hildegard," almost eight-years old, by a previous marriage. Anne Louise and Gretchen also stayed with me and Mom quite a bit, and I grew very close to my Aunt Anne Louise. She adored me and I her. I remember how she got all dressed up and dressed me up, and we'd go downtown to Nuremberg and shop or just walk around in stores. She also took me to the park many times while Mom was working.

My Aunt Erna decided one day to go visit her husband who was stationed in Wildflecken. He was to be sent to the front real soon, so Hildegard went to stay with her paternal grandparents who were older people in their late 60's. They were my aunt's ex in-laws.

Then, the most horrible of horrible happened while she was gone. There was a severe air attack taking place over Nuremberg, and there was not much time to warn the people so lots of them could not make it to the bomb shelters; instead, they took cover in their apartment building basements. Hildegard, my little cousin, and her grandparents were among those staying behind and not trying to get to the shelter. Hildegard was very afraid and cried. She wanted to go to the shelter. Liesl, a young girl also in the basement said she was going to make a run for the shelter, so Hildegard wanted to go with her, but her grandparents said "No!" and that she would have to stay with them. It was a terrible attack. The whole street was almost completely wiped out. A bomb was dropped on the complex where Hildegard and her grandparents were trapped below. One hundred thirty-three people perished that night on that street to include my little cousin and her grandparents. Liesl got out and made it to the shelter. She told us later how Hildegard cried and was so afraid.

Food was now being rationed and many homes were without electricity and water. The City of Nuremberg had a terrible shortage of bread and called out to other cities in Germany for help for most of our bakeries were without water and wood to fire up the bread baking ovens. They also ran out of caskets for the dead; they had to put bodies into bags for burial. The smell of burning fires lingered over the city. So many of our beautiful architectural structures were demolished. Beautiful medieval art all gone as well.

Lots of times when we emerged from the shelter we would see many dead people lying in the streets; those that did not make it to the shelter on time. I remember seeing a little girl crying as she bent over her mother, shaking her head saying "Wake up Mommy, wake up!" There were tears streaming down her little face as her neighbor tried to pull her away. She kept saying, "Please get up Mommy!" Her mommy would never get up again; she was dead!

The Russian troops were now entering Germany from the East and so were the Americans. They had crossed the bridge at the Rhine River into Remagen. Time went on and it was Christmas. Little did we know that it was to be our last one, our last one in our home and our possessions all gone? My Mom baked a few cookies and I got a new doll and some new items for my doll house that was so beautiful and I loved playing with so much. It was also a very spiritual Christmas with songs and going to Midnight Mass. My Dad was not here because he was somewhere on the front. People were praying for peace and that this terrible war would end soon. People were already getting so sad and weary. We got the news the day after Christmas that my Dad was wounded and lay in some military hospital. He had fought in the cold of Russia and became wounded. I wanted Dad to come home and take care of us.

Another air raid and another strike again and then on January 2, 1945 came a big one; a total bomb out. We went to the shelter as usual. It was nighttime and very, very cold. I just remember having to get up out of my nice warm bed to go out into the cold night. That would be the last night I got to sleep in my bed, play with my new and old toys (my beautiful doll house) or eat another meal at our table. I'll never forget coming out of that shelter and seeing nothing but fire all around us.

By some miracle, the shelter was the only building left in the whole street; everything else was gone. Our apartment building was burning from top to bottom. Everything we owned, all gone! All we had left was what we had on our backs and the contents of our suitcase and shoulder bag, but most importantly we had our lives and God meant for us to live.

In order for us to escape this inferno, we all had to run through it at the point where the fire was at its lowest. My Mom pulled her scarf down over her face, then threw the blanket over me and then we ran as fast as we could along with other people. Some people's clothes actually caught fire as well as their hair. The smell was horrible; the smoke burned my nose and throat. We stepped over rubble. Burning wood and bricks were scattered everywhere. Everyone tried to get away from the intense heat and find a safe place.

Mom and I made our way to my Aunt's place, Mom's older sister Erna. She lived across town so we walked and walked until we reached her apartment where she lived with the two youngest sisters, Aunt Anne Louise and Gretchen and, of course, Hansl, the youngest brother. Luckily, their apartment building was still intact. I felt so sorry for my poor Mom. She stood there holding my hand, suitcase and bag next to her on the floor. She rang the doorbell and then started crying as my aunt appeared who also started crying. The loss of her only child was still bearing down on her. My Mom's loss and mine of all of our belongings, my Dad away in some hospital lying there wounded had caught up with us all. Aunt Erna hugged us both and told us to come in. We were at that point pretty much homeless.

Mine and Mom's new home consisted of a small bedroom that Hansl had occupied up to that point, but he was glad to give it up for his sister and her little girl so he took the couch in the living room for his bed.

Our room had a single bed, a night stand and a dresser, but we were very grateful to have that much. This was a time when we had to stick together and help each other. Not any of us had very much to eat. There was very little bread and sometimes that was very hard to chew. Water was rationed also. I played with all the other children from the apartment complex in between bombardments that were still happening.

One day as I came in from playing outside, I heard screaming and yelling coming down from the second floor. It was coming from two females. I recognized immediately it was my aunt's voice, so curiously I stuck my head around the stairway banister and saw my Aunt Anne Louise in a heated argument with "Frau Mueller" who lived on the second floor. Just as I got upstairs and walked up on them, my aunt was holding an 11 x 14 oil painting of Adolph Hitler that hung on the wall at the entrance of Frau Mueller's apartment. She had removed it from the wall and holding it up above her head threatened the wide-eyed, shocked Frau Mueller that she was going to smash it. Frau Mueller, whose husband was a high ranking Nazi, kept telling my aunt to put the portrait back on the wall, but my aunt refused and called Hitler all sorts of names such as "that Murderer, that War Criminal, etc."

Frau Mueller at that point threatened my Aunt Anne Louise to have her shot, but that was the last straw for my aunt. She raised the portrait high again, raising her right knee, and tried to burst right through the middle of Hitler's face. Not having been successful with her plan of destruction, she threw the portrait on the floor and started jumping up and down with her feet. I saw the shock and horror on Mueller's face throwing both hands up, then shaking her finger at my aunt she shouted, "I will have you sent to a concentration camp as soon as I contact my husband or the SS Authorities. No sooner than she had made these horrible threats, I saw my aunt leap at her. That's when Frau Mueller retreated to her apartment, slamming the door. My Aunt Anne Louise turned around to head downstairs when she saw me standing there. I was wide-eyed and shaking in my shoes. She took me by the hand then she pulled me up close as she sat down with me on the top step sobbing endlessly.

While holding me close to her, she was saying between sobs, "how many more people have to die, lose everything or starve. Why, Why, Why? - - all because of this crazy maniac." She was crying and saying all sorts of bad things about Adolph, but in those days there were not many who did not have this mutual opinion of him. I, too, started crying and looking up at my beloved aunt, (She was my favorite) I cried, "But I don't want them to put you in a concentration camp!"

The city's food supply had now become very scarce and there were food lines where old men and women as well as children of all ages lined up for food which was distributed by Nazi officers. Sometimes the supply became totally exhausted and the remainder of people waiting in line had to remain there until the supply was replenished. On one such day after my mother stood in line for a long time, as she came upon the server, the bowl of soup she received had turned cold and smelled sour. Mom looked around and saw an armed SS in his uniform. He was standing holding both hands clasped behind him. I remember looking at his big belly sticking out, adorned with a wide leather belt from which hung a revolver on one side. It really scared me just looking at him, but my Mother was very angry as she headed towards him, the small bowl of soup in one hand and holding my hand with the other.

She asked him to smell of the soup. He sort of nodded his head down towards the soup, then smiled and said with his arrogant voice, "Smells fine." I could then see the anger in my Mother's face, tears filling her eyes as she emptied the soup in front of his feet. By then, her voice became loud as she angrily replied, "I have stood for hours in line for this lousy sour soup that you expect me to feed to my child. The SS's face turned red and his beady eyes turned to two small lines. As he stepped back, his right hand reached for his beltline pulling out a revolver, he replied in a blood chilling tone. "Shut up or I will shoot you right here on the spot." At that time two soldiers came walking up and stopped him from pulling the gun on my mother. One of the soldiers then pulled my mother over and told her to go on before something tragic would happen. He was carrying a backpack which he pulled off. He told her to wait a second. He reached inside and pulled out a half of a pack of pumpernickel bread and handed it to her. She did not want to take it, but he insisted she take it. We then went back to my aunt's apartment where she brewed some hot tea from a tea bag that had seen more than one cup of brewing and we ate our pumpernickel bread. Anything tastes good when you are hungry.

At this time, most all of the city was without water and electricity. People hovered in the streets over burning fires that they built from make shift outdoor stoves made from bricks and rocks. It kept them warn and helped to warm up some of the foods like soup or teas or whatever there was that could be or needed to be warmed. It was all a very sad scene; some of the people were wandering along through rubble as if looking for things. Some would walk the streets as though they were in some kind of trance; their minds seemed to be in another place, at another time. Some were teary eyed, but they all looked so tired and weary with so much pain, so much sorrow, and, for some, so many losses.

I remember thinking why is all this misery happening: why did there have to be a war and all this pain thrown at people? This seemed to be bearing on my young mind. I thought about it each and every day , praying mornings and nights, asking God that he would make it all end and let everyone live in peace and be happy again. I remember wishing for a nice warm place to live with a soft warm featherbed to sleep in and lots and lots of good warm food to eat, especially lots of hot cream of wheat (my favorite breakfast food cooked with milk, sugar and butter then sprinkled with cinnamon and sugar). For now, we did well to get a piece of bread and some tea to drink. Meanwhile, the Battle of the Bulge was over. It had been a last effort of the German Army to conquer a senseless war.

Our soldiers were tired and cold with their spirits having sunk to a very low point. They headed for home knowing the war was lost. All they wanted was to be home with their families. Unfortunately, this is not how the big Nazi leaders felt. They instructed all the SS Troops to put a rope around any soldier's neck that left the front and hang him or them from the next available tree.

My father was worried about us. He knew the cities had been heavily bombed so he asked for an emergency leave of absence for a few days in order to come home and evacuate us to the country where the bombing seemed less intense and life much safer. At first his request was declined, but after lots of pleading with his commander, he was granted a few days leave. He arrived in Nuremberg around the first of February, and as he told me several years later, how saddened he was upon his arrival and how his heart ached when he saw what happened to our beautiful, beloved city of Nuremberg.

Nuremberg, a city with a history dating back 1000 years. Emperor Karl who lived in the Old Castle built on the city's highest point, which towered over the city, now it was partially demolished. The poets and artists such as Hans Albrecht Duerer, world renowned, they, too, lived here once. Now, all the beautiful medieval architecture of buildings, statues and churches, mostly in Gothic styles, were totally or partially destroyed.

Now there was burning rubble everywhere. Nuremberg has always been known as the most romantic and intimate city of Germany, very picturesque, having poets who lived here and those that didn't loved to visit. There were beautiful parks with monuments, fountains and rivers that ran alongside. The outskirts of the city had beautiful forests in which we used to go for long walks on weekends. My grandparents usually went along and sometimes other family members including aunts, uncles, nieces and even family friends. We would carry little pails and pick blueberries when they came in season or mushrooms. Sometimes were rode bicycles. I was once given a ride in a bike basket which was ridden by one of my parents. On our way we would stop in one of the "Gasthaus Garten" (an outdoor or sidewalk garden restaurant). We ate there sometimes or stopped for a refreshing cool drink. Most of the "Gasthaus" had a band playing german folk music. There was also a beautiful lake called the "Dutzen Teich." We would rent one of the boats or paddle boats. The lake was near the then "Reichspartei Stadium" where Hitler came into power. He had this built so when he came to Nuremberg, he held his speeches in the stadium. That is where the parades were held.

My Dad told me that one day when he and my Mother went to ride their bikes on the outskirts of Nuremberg then suddenly there came an entourage of cabriolet cars. As they headed towards the stadium in one of the cars was Adolph Hitler; of course, my parents stepped off their bikes and looked on. They said that Adolph Hitler looked at them and saluted. They had to salute back with the well-known then and everyday "Heil Hitler" used by everyone.

Nuremberg had become the "Reichs Hauptstadt." (Hitler's capital city for speeches). He held big speeches at the "Partei Stadium" with soldiers marching to the sound of a military band. There used to be lots of marching bands during the victorious years of Hitler, nothing but ongoing war. I remember looking down from our apartment window distressed by the marching soldiers as they went by. Now, there was nothing left but rubble and misery on the beautiful streets in which my Dad had grown up. Now there were bulldozers pushing bricks, wood and steel out of the way. A wooden plaque of some sort was erected on a stand. It read "60 people have lost their lives that once lived here."

It was the apartment complex where my Dad had grown up. As my Dad had often remembered, in Hitler's words once proclaimed in one of his speeches, "If the enemy wants Germany, he'll have to walk over the dead. We will never give up; this is Total War until the end." Does that not sound like the words of a crazy man?

Upon my Dad's return, when he had finally found us after searching the homes, apartments of several relatives, most of which did not exist any longer. He was stunned. He had seen his share of pain, heartache and misery during his five years of fighting at the front but when he arrived here and saw all of the destruction, he sobbed bitterly. The City of Nuremberg had suffered fifty-nine air attacks.

CHAPTER III

My Dad pulled us close to his chest and held us tightly as the three of us sobbed. Still, we all felt a wonderful feeling of relief and happiness to have him there with us, even if it was only temporarily. My aunts and young uncle were also happy to see him; after all, he was a soldier and gave all of us a feeling of protection because from day to day, we all lived in fear for our lives.

The day after my Dad's initial arrival was fairly peaceful and we began making preparations and planning for our evacuation; however, the second day turned out quite the opposite. That morning around 11 o'clock we heard shrieking sirens and warning of an oncoming air attack. It seemed to be coming from the Northern sky. Obviously, we had all stepped outside, my Dad holding my hand. There they came like a swarm of black birds but sounding like thousands of bumble bees, but we had no time to make it to the shelter down the street, so we headed for the basement of the apartment building. Everyone in our family plus some other tenants who were in the same situation with each person carrying the necessities, change of clothes, first aid items and finally food and water.

There was an older man in the group, Herr Hoffmann; he was in his mid fifties and sort of in charge of the building. Each building had one person that was appointed for everyone and their needs. Herr Hoffmann seemed sort of upset yet he was trying to keep himself calm as he announced that the planes were dropping phosphorus bombs on top of the roofs. These bombs would cause first to erupt in the attics and naturally ignite the rest of the building. My Dad took my twenty-year old uncle with him and they made their way up to the attic where there stood huge buckets of sand. They then grabbed a shovel and started throwing the sand onto the burning flames. Suddenly there was a tremendous noise being heard that rocked our entire building. A bomb had been dropped on the roof of the apartment building next door to ours. My Dad, having trained as an ammunition and demolition expert, recognized immediately the type of bomb that had been dropped. He grabbed Hansl and motioned to him to head back down to the basement as the whole building started to sway. There was much shaking and glass from the windows bursting; wood seemed to be flying everywhere. A beam came down striking my uncle on one side of his head. Blood was coming from his wound and he fell on the steps that led down. My Dad picked him up and carried him down, holding him over his shoulder. He finally made it down to the basement where, with the help of my Mom and Aunt Erna, they cleaned his wound and put a bandage around his head.

After the air raid was over, an ambulance carried him to a nearby hospital. I should mention that the reason my uncle was not drafted into the military and didn't have to participate in World War II was because he suffered from epilepsy. Of course, this head injury didn't help matters. He was kept in the hospital for several days and kept under observation as he did suffer from a concussion and skull fracture.

This day had turned into another terrible air raid where many people lost their lives and many were wounded. Children were out in the streets calling for their mothers, crying terribly, with mothers calling out to their children as well. They had once again become separated in all the turmoil; it was truly a holocaust.

The radio announced that 200,000 people had lost their lives the night before in the city of Dresden. The city had become overloaded with refugees that came from the Eastern part of Germany which by then had been taken by the Russian troops. The mass of people had grown to five million. They had told the people to go into a big stadium located in the center of the city. Unfortunately, it was bombed and 200,000 people in it lost their lives. At the end of the war, it was told that 8 million people lost their lives; 5 million civilians and 3 million soldiers.

When Hansl got out of the hospital, he and my youngest aunts, Anne Louise and Gretel, went to live with their Dad and new stepmother. My Dad got our few things together so that he could get my aunt Erna, my Mom and me evacuated to the country before another bad air strike would occur. Maybe the next time we wouldn't be so lucky. My Dad only had a few days of furlough, so we packed our few belongings and headed to the train station. We got on a train and headed out of Nuremberg towards the country. We rode on the train for a while when suddenly it came to an abrupt stop. I nearly fell out of my seat with my Dad grabbing me just in time. The conductor came through and announced that everyone had to get off of the train. The railroad tracks had been badly bombed and were badly damaged. Everyone then got off and started, or rather, continued their journey on foot. What else could we do? It was not easy carrying a suitcase and other baggage including taking care of a little girl that sooner or later would become tired and need to be carried.

I must say at this point, my Dad was really a very smart, practical and intelligent man who always seemed to come up with a solution for any problem. We then made our way to a farmer's house where Dad saw a small pull wagon made out of wood and it even had sides on it made from wooden slats. It would be perfect to hold all our baggage and I could sit on top of the suitcase and get a free ride. I was getting excited at the thought of riding on top of this cute little wooden wagon.

My Dad did not have any money to buy the wagon, but he had an extra pair of military combat boots with him that the farmer was willing to trade for. I felt like we had just made one big purchase. My Dad then loaded the wagon and then sat me on top. He pulled as my Mom and Erna walked alongside and helped to push. I felt like a princess sitting on her throne. I enjoyed looking at the beautiful country side; it felt great looking at the wide open fields and trees. After leaving the rubble of the bombed out city behind, where smoke and other horrible smells had remained prevalent, it was good to be away.

I was still very cold and as my Dad was hurrying along, all of a sudden there were planes flying over us. One came down low and started shooting at us with machine guns. We ran to the side of the road where there were some shrubs and a ditch. We lay down with my Dad lying on top of me and my Mom trying to shield us from bullets. I was screaming and crying so hard as I shook all over. My Mom and Dad had a really hard time trying to calm me down. I just knew they were going to kill us with all those bullets that were flying all around us. I believe in "Guardian Angels," and we had one with us that day and every day thereafter.

The planes flew off into the distance and we went back to our wagon and resumed our journey. We then came up on a plow and horse and two women out in the field. The horse was dead. It had been shot by one of the planes. The two women also seemed very upset after having survived but watched the poor horse losing his life. We followed them into the Village Bruehl. That was our new destination since the train did not make it to our previous planned destination where my Dad's cousin lived on a farm. We were to stay with them, but it was too far to walk on foot and my Dad had to get back to the front so he would not be considered AWOL.

One of the women told us about a farmhouse where we may be able to find a place to stay. The farmer's wife had recently died and he needed some help in the house and also with the farm work which consisted of milking and feeding all kinds of fowl and animals, cleaning out stalls, etc. My Dad then met the farmer and introduced his family. The man had seemed tired and weary looking. My Dad discussed several things with him and they came to an agreement that my Mom and Aunt Erna would perform chores around the house and farm in exchange for food and board. My Mom and I shared a bedroom and my Aunt had a very small room with a single bed to sleep on, but it meant a lot to us because we really had nowhere else to go. Our bedrooms were located upstairs and from our bedroom window, you could see out into the main street of the village. There were only other farm houses, a school house, church, two small stores and a pub. Most all of the farmers here lived totally off their land. They raised their own hogs, beef, chicken, ducks and even rabbits. They made their own butter and cheese and had fresh milk daily. Also, in the spring and summer, they had a large garden and its harvest was canned for the cold months of winter. They grew barley, oats and wheat as well so all they really needed to buy was sugar and coffee.

It was getting late by the time we were settled in and had our things put away. The farmer invited us to take part in the evening meal; a thought that welcomed each and every one of us for it had been a while since we had drink or food and we were all very hungry. My Dad expressed his appreciation for the invitation and we all sat down to eat with the meal consisting of homemade potato soup, German country rye bread, butter, cheese, country ham and a glass of milk. None of us could remember when we had had this much food to eat at one meal and especially in such abundance. After dinner, my Mom along with my Aunt Erna washed up the dirty dishes and helped the farmer's old mother who also lived there clean up the kitchen. We then returned to our rooms and fell exhausted into our beds and into a deep sleep.

The shrill crowing of a very loud-sounding rooster woke me up the next morning. My parents were still asleep so I tiptoed out of bed and curiously looked around. The furniture was all handmade out of wood and painted with colorful folklore. It seemed to be made of very heavy wood. I walked over to the window, pulling the curtain aside and got a good look down into the street. I saw a farmer go by sitting on top of a wagon that was being pulled by two oxen. Having been raised in the city all of my years, this was something totally new and interesting for me.

I heard my parents waking up and soon we were getting our clothes on to go down and meet our new surroundings. I heard my Dad tell my Mom that he needed to get back soon because he was already running out of time and would be considered AWOL if he did not leave today.

I heard my Mom telling him that she wished he could stay, and I felt my eyes filling up with tears and I had a horrible pain in my stomach. The very thought of my dear Daddy leaving again and going back to fight a senseless war was horrible, so I just cut loose crying my heart out saying , "Daddy, please stay. I will miss you so much when you're not with me and I am so afraid. He picked me up, wiped my tears and kissed my forehead saying, "Don't cry my angel girl. I will be back soon and I will never leave you again." Remember, Daddy has to go in order that all this will be over soon and we can go back home. Say your prayers every night and remember that I love you very much, with all my heart. I will think about you and your Mom each and every day. That sort of calmed me down and we all went downstairs where my aunt was helping the old Mother set the table for breakfast.

The old lady in the house had been somewhat taking care of things in the house since the farmer's wife had died, but she was elderly and could not get around anymore due to some problems in her hip and legs. She really welcomed the extra help that she was getting from my Mom and my aunt. We sat down and ate a delicious morning breakfast consisting of hot oatmeal, white home baked hard rolls with butter and apple jelly. We also had coffee and milk; it had been a long time since we had this much for breakfast. Now the smell of the country was a bit different from the smell of the city. It smelled like a mixture of warm milk and cow manure as was the case in most farm houses.

He kitchen usually led to a stall where the cows stayed that were milked mornings and evenings. Maybe this was just the setup for lack of space or just plain convenience. I never really found this out. It was kept very clean with a farmhand removing the soiled straw every morning and evening and it being wheelbarrowed out to the middle of the farmyard where

It was put in a large pile and later taken to the fields and used as fertilizer. The floor was also swept on a daily basis.

I decided to stroll outside to explore our new home, looking at barns and other buildings. An old plow was being hitched up to a horse that was taken to a field for plowing. I didn't stay out too long as the morning was still pretty chilly. My Dad had planned on leaving hat day sometime after lunch. I followed him up to the room and watched him pack up his few things. I felt terribly sad and wanted to cry again, but I tried really hard not to in order to make it easier for my Dad to leave. I walked over by the window and looked down. I noticed that some of the children were playing. It was Saturday and there wasn't any school so they were playing next to a small creek. I looked them over very anxiously. Somehow they looked different from the children in the city. To me, they looked country!

The girls wore their dresses much longer than we did and they all looked so much bigger and healthier. They seemed to have big fat rosy cheeks. I asked my Dad if I could go down and play and he said, "Yes." I went down and introduced myself and met them. They were looking at me just as curiously as I had looked at them. They all seemed real nice and invited me to play tossing a ball. Unfortunately, as they say, "There is one in every bunch!" One of the little girls didn't seem to like me and made it obvious she didn't want me to play. She got downright ugly and hateful with me and called me a "city slicker: or something on that order because I came from the big city. I looked at her and told her that was too bad that I was going to play anyway. She then gave me a push and then I gave her a big push and backwards into the creek she fell.

Of course, the weather was still cold and she was now all wet. The other kids were laughing, but as I saw the window above me opening and my Dad looking down at me very seriously, ordering me to come inside and upstairs immediately. I knew I was in trouble. My Dad had actually seen everything so he knew I didn't start the fight, just finished it. He said that I should not have pushed the girl into the water. He told me later he hated to have to spank me before going back to the front but that would be only one of two spankings that I ever received from my Dad during my entire life. He had to discipline me; discipline in those days was a very important issue in a child's life. I had been brought up to obey and respect my parents and all grownups; back talking was not allowed or tolerated.

My Dad left that afternoon; little did we know we would not see him until four years later. He hitchhiked a ride with a transport truck part of the way and then went on foot, and finally hitchhiking some more until he arrived at his military unit. I really missed my Dad terribly and cried for him most every night. My Mom and my Aunt Erna both worked very hard every day in the kitchen, cleaning the house and on the farm and even in the fields.

Planting season began and things really got busy. It seemed that after my Dad left the farmer didn't seem as nice any more, and he put more and more chores on to my Mom and my Aunt. Then, all of a sudden, ham and other meats were cut out of our meals. He claimed he couldn't afford to feed us meat unless he could get something of value in return. He found out that my Mom had a few pieces of jewelry left, and so it was traded off for country ham, eggs and other so called luxury foods, but they continued to work just as hard as well. There was a Polish farm-hand employed that was trying to come on to my Mom and that caused a lot of commotion. Of course, he denied it, saying she came on to him.

Things were getting tense. The fear of the foreign invasion grew among men, women and children. We knew it was coming very soon, but we didn't know whether it would be the American allies or the Russians, hoping all the while it would be the former. Everyone feared the Russian troops. They had spread a very bad and scary reputation all over Germany. They had raped young girls age fourteen and women as old as their mid or late seventies. They stayed drunk on Vodka and were wild. Not only one but several men would rape these poor women. Word got out that tanks were coming toward the neighboring village. One of the boys that I had played with told me if you lay on the ground and put your ear down close, we would be able to hear the vibration of the tanks. I remember lying down with the other children pressing my ear close to the ground.

It was the beginning of April and spring seemed to be coming up all around us. It was the day before my birthday and the big tanks arrived into our village. Thank God, they were Americans as everyone sighed with relief, but yet everyone was afraid and stayed inside their homes behind locked doors and windows. There was not a civilian anywhere in sight; only Americans in their jeeps and trucks or sitting and standing on top of their tanks. I was fascinated and I didn't feel the slightest fear. Something told me all of this was very good and things would get better.

My curiosity seemed at its peak and I just had to go see all those soldiers. Their uniforms were so different from my Dad's and they all seemed to be chewing continuously on what, I couldn't figure out because they didn't swallow anything but still kept chewing. It seemed very strange in those days because we had never heard of chewing gum. I went up to them. They spoke to me but I couldn't understand anything they said. I just smiled and they smiled. Then one of them picked me up and sat me on top of that big tank. Boy, I thought I was being crowned a princess sitting on top of her throne with all her armored knights below and around her! I decided then I really liked those "nice Americans." They gave me all kinds of good things – candies, cookies, etc. I thought I was in dreamland. None of the other kids or adults dared to come out of their homes. My Mom, who by now had started to miss me, looked out the window and nearly passed out when she saw me among all those soldiers sitting on top of a tank with them being our enemies on top of that. When she finally caught her breath and found her voice, she called my name. She later told me that I smiled big and waived at her and held up some goodies.

The GIs each was pointing to themselves, telling me their names. Then they pointed at me and I understood that they wanted to know my name. I smiled and said, "Helga." "Hello, Helga" said those smiling GIs and then I had to laugh. I felt so important and honored all the while my Mom kept calling me to come upstairs right away. They understood so one of them lifted me gently off the tank and handed me all my acquired goodies to take home. I then waved good bye and knew that I would see my newly made friends again. I felt good about them and had no fear whatsoever. Somehow I felt a big relief inside and thought everything would be alright. This was my very first encounter with the American people. Our so called enemy!

I went upstairs to face what I knew would be a scolding from Mom and that was just what I got. She gave me this big long lecture about going out there and putting myself in such danger, but I kept saying "But Mom, they are not mean; they are so nice and look what they gave me!" When I grow up, I am going to America and get married to one of them."

I think that put a seed of desire in my little heart and brain; from that day forth, this would be something I would be doing one day. That seed never stopped growing. It was from that day forward that I was fascinated with anything and everything that pertained to AMERICA; it literally became my most inner desire to come and live in this great country someday.

The next day the Americans were all over the village. Mom had calmed down and after being reassured the

Americans did not hurt anyone, she agreed to let me go outside to play. Other villagers too were drawn by curiosity and came out of their homes Most had resumed their normal chores and activities. Living on farms as most of them did, they had to take care of their animals and all that went along with it.

I strolled out and looked at all that strange equipment, jeeps, trucks and tanks. With all of those soldiers being dressed in khaki uniforms, I then recognized some familiar faces that were standing close to the tank on which I had sat on top of the day before. They discovered me about the same time waving me over and saying, "Hello Helga, come here." I hurried over and one of the GIs picked me up again and sat me on top of the tank. I didn't see any kids from the neighboring farms come over. I think they were still afraid with some standing off in the distance and others looking out from their windows.

It was April 11th, being my birthday. That day I learned my first American song, "You Are My Sunshine!" I think those GIs had as much fun with me as I had with them. One of the soldiers played the song on his mouth harp and the other sang along. Soon they had me singing with them over and over until I sang the whole song by myself. I was so excited I could sing a song in English. I went around the rest of that day singing, "You are my sunshine, my only sunshine!"

One of the GIs whose name was Bill could speak a little German. He called me over to him holding an egg in his hand. He said, "Can you get us more of these from the farm?" He smiled and said that I would get more candies and other goodies for doing that. I said "OK" and took off. I went to the farmer and told him I needed a basket full of eggs and he needed to give me as many as he could. I also told him that would keep them happy and they would not make any trouble for him, so off he went and filled a medium-size wicker basket with eggs. I could tell by the look on his face that didn't sit too well, but when I pointed cautiously to the tank, he handed the basket over to me. My new friends were thrilled when I brought them the eggs. They were the only safe fresh food they would eat for fear that other foods may have been poisoned. I am sure they were all getting tired of canned goods and seafood rations.

Of course, by now, I had a good little trading business going on. Life started back to its normal routine with everyone pretty much being used to the Americans now. They caused no harm or trouble to anyone. My Mom, Aunt and I would usually go out for walks in the evenings. As we walked to the outskirts of the village on this one particular evening, we noticed the smell of budding trees and flowers filling the air with a delightful fragrance. We came up on a couple of American soldiers who were also taking a walk. They smiled and greeted us as well. Suddenly, out of nowhere came a German Luftwaffe plane and started shooting down as they flew over the village. What happened next amazed my Mom, my Aunt Erna and, of course, me. The two soldiers grabbed us, one me and my Mom and the other my aunt. They then made us lay on the ground with each one lying protectively on top of us. They were risking giving up their lives in order to save ours. We were all so shaken, yet we could not thank those two soldiers enough for what they had done.

All of West Germany was now occupied by the Americans; the eastern part being occupied by Russia. Actually, when they invaded Berlin, it was divided into four sectors; American, Russian, English and French. Later, the French and English pulled out and it was only West and East Berlin with American and Russian occupation. We felt so fortunate that we lived in the Southwestern part of

Germany totally taken by the Americans. What a difference it made. Nuremberg had been taken by the 7th Army on April 21, 1945.

Life on the farm was getting harder now that all of Mom's and my Aunt's jewelry was gone. There was no more meat of any kind; most of the time potatoes, some vegetable and maybe once a week we'd get eggs. Mom and Aunt Erna were sent out to do work in the fields. Then, when they came in they had to take care of chores with milking cows, kitchen work, etc. The farmer was not making life very easy for us, so Mom and Aunt Erna decided to head back to Nuremberg to my Aunt's apartment, and that's if it was still standing!

One morning after packing up our few belongings, we left on foot. I waved goodbye at some of my new friends that I had made, and we headed out of the village. We ran upon a young man about seventeen years of age. He said he had been staying with relatives here in Brueghel and now was also heading back to Nuremberg. We figured he went to the country as well to keep from being drafted by Hitler. He asked if he could join up and walk back along with us; we told him that he could.

CHAPTER IV

BACK ON FOOT TO
NUREMBERG

There was no train running due to the demolished railroad. No buses ran; our only option was to walk on foot. It was approximately 35 to 40 miles to Nuremberg. We walked all day taking short breaks and eating the sandwiches that Mom and Aunt Erna had made and brought along. Mom and my aunt had blisters on their feet. Moms were so bad that she took her shoes off and walked with bare feet. We were dead tired and it started to get dark. All of a sudden, there came a convoy of American trucks and jeeps with one of the last trucks pulling over. Our hearts then started to pound in our chest when a black soldier got out of his truck and walked towards us. He was very tall and very dark. His eyes were big and the white in them shone in the near darkness as the moon surfaced and reflected on his face. He looked us over and said something that none of us understood. He looked down at Mom's feet and mumbled something else. He then motioned us to follow him to the truck, picking me up and seating me in the back. He motioned to Karl, our new companion, to also get up in there, he then picked Mom up and let Karl help her get in the truck with my aunt being last. He finally got up in the truck himself and told us to lie down in the floor of the truck. Then he covered us with some kind of heavy tarpaulin. We thought he had probably done this so no one would see or discover us. I'm sure that he would have gotten in trouble if he were caught transporting civilians on an Army vehicle. He then got in front of the truck and started it in motion. We rode for a short distance when the truck pulled over and stopped. He got out and walked up to a house speaking a little German and asking he woman in the house for a pan of water. He came over to the truck and had Mom to get out. As he was helping her down, he asked her to sit on the step that led inside of the lady's house. He told her to put her feet into the water. She sat there while he walked back to the truck and came back with a first aid kit. Mom's feet were so bad they bled in places. He bent down and washed her feet off with soap and patted them dry. He then applied some sort of ointment that came out of a tube and then put bandages on both feet.

I had watched this episode from the back of the truck with my aunt and Karl looking at each other in disbelief and as to say, "And this is the enemy!" What a kind and compassionate soldier this was. He took big chances of getting himself in trouble in order to help us. He thanked the lady that gave him the pan with water, soap and a towel, and finally helping Mom back into the truck and we all lay down again and were covered up with the tarp. The truck then headed on towards Nuremberg with him letting us out on the outskirts of town because he was going in a different direction. Mom thanked him; we all did. He was our "Angel of Rescue" in a time when we much needed help. Karl also headed in a different direction after he told us "good bye" and we all wished each other luck.

We didn't have too much farther to walk and soon we arrived at my Aunt Erna's apartment complex that luckily was still there. Her apartment was on the first floor so we had no stairs to climb. We went inside the apartment and sighed a sigh of relief. We then fell into bed and into deep sleep. It was so good being back, especially now that the war was officially over. We slept for ten hours, got up, cleaned up and put on fresh clothes. I had looked out the window thinking here too there had been a lot that had changed. There was a complex of apartments on each side and at one end stood a large school building that was presently occupied by the U.S. Armed Forces so soldiers and their equipment were everywhere. As I mentioned before, Nuremberg was officially taken on April 21, 1945 after four days of resistance. The American troops had celebrated their victory by performing marches through the streets of Nuremberg. They consisted of the 7th Army and the 15th US Corps that were led by Generals Patch and Hayslip. The soldiers performed and celebrated in their honor. By now, it was mid-May and they had settled well into different buildings such as school houses, hotel and even a German facility called Soldier's Field (Merrell Barracks) which held a large number of military personnel. It became the home, too, for many GIs while stationed over there for many years to come.

Nuremberg had been destroyed immensely with 90% of all the beautiful buildings being down or having been damaged. It was a terrible sight to see what had happened to such a beautiful city. We had all suffered so many losses, family members, relatives and friends. Many, including ourselves, lost their homes and all possessions there in. We got the bad news that my Great Grandparents Meyer, the ones that used to take care of me, lost their lives on

March 16, 1945, just before the end of the war. I began to cry and Mom had a hard time calming me down. Those two people were the kindest, sweetest people and it was so sad to think that they were not around any longer. Five hundred seventeen people lost their lives that night, attacked by the Royal Air Force consisting of 275 Bombers Type Lancaster and 16 Maquitos destined for bombing Nuremberg. We found my paternal Grandparents. They also lost their home but found a small apartment to move into. My grandfather, who also fought in Russia with the German Infantry, had just returned back home. He escaped from captivity and walked on foot through the forest in deep snow for many miles until coming into Germany where he got help from different people with food and shelter until he made it back home to Nuremberg. He suffered frost bite on his toes and feet but thank god he got back safe.

My Uncle Robert {Dad's younger brother) however was still gone. He was a soldier in the German Navy. Mom and I would go and visit my grandparents now and then with everywhere we went going on foot because that was the only way to get around. There was no transportation. The street cars were not in working order with most having been destroyed. No one seemed to have anything; there was little food and drink, and I stayed hungry most of the time.

One day we went over to my grandparent's house in hopes that they might have a little extra food they could share, but unfortunately they were not at home so we left to go back to my Aunt's place. I started to cry; it hurt Mom terribly to see me cry because I was hungry and she didn't have anything to give me. She was holding me by the hand and tried to calm me down when we came by a Catholic Church. Suddenly, I looked up at Mom and said, "Let's go inside Mom and pray to God. Maybe he will give us something to eat." She went inside with me. We dipped our hands into the Holy Water making the "Sign of the Cross" and headed towards the front of the church close to the altar where we knelt down on a bench and we prayed. Mom was crying, but I kept saying, "Please God, help us, we are hungry and we have no food." At this point, a priest walked up touching Mom's shoulder. He said, "Are you troubled my daughter?" Mom told him everything and that I had suggested coming inside to pray to God for help. The priest looked at us with a compassionate look on his face. Then, he pointed in the direction of the altar and said, "Your child led you to the right place."

The nuns back at the convent made a large pot of potato soup so come with me and you both shall be fed. We followed him through the back of the church into the convent where the nuns lived. They sat us down at the large table and gave us a bowel of wonderful hot soup, a slice of rye bread and a cup of hot tea. After the blessing, we gave thanks and enjoyed this delicious meal. I looked up at Mom and said, "You see, God did hear our prayer." Mom gave me a hug.

There were many days of meager meals; we all had lost weight. The City of Nuremberg started to get cleaned up. Boys and men ages 14 to 65 and women ages 15 to 50 were asked to bring picks, shovels, wheel barrows and other tools that were available. They met at the market place where different groups were formed and then sent out to different job sites for the cleanup process with everyone that was able to help participating

Food was now rationed with the schools giving out hot oatmeal or hot cream of wheat cereal every morning. It was furnished by the Americans. We all looked forward to these hot cereals; for us who had such little food for so long, it was quite a treat. Mom's two younger sisters, Anne Louise and Gretchen and her younger brother Hansel had moved back into the apartment with us. They had been living with my maternal grandfather and his new wife. They had been sort of hurt by their father's sudden matrimony so soon after their beloved mother's death, so they wanted to come live with us. They, too, felt the extreme shortage of food supply. It was fun having them around. They were always playing some kind of game with me, but they argued a lot. Hans picked at the girls and, of course, they didn't like it and repaid him with additional pranks.

It's been a very long time now since we have heard anything from my Dad. We wondered about his whereabouts and if he were okay. Some rumors had it that he was a Prisoner of War in French captivity. I missed him terribly and wished daily for his return. We struggled daily for food and drink. One midmorning, Mom, my three aunts and my uncle started out walking towards the outskirts of Nuremberg looking for some farmland in search for food. We were now into the season where vegetables were getting ready for harvesting. After walking for a while, we ran up on a field in which grew some nice heads of cabbage and carrots. We started to pull some up and put into my Mom's and Aunt Erna's shopping bags when suddenly out of nowhere came a US Army jeep with two soldiers. They stopped and got out walking toward us. One of them spoke some German and asked what we were doing. My Mom then looked them in the eyes and said, "My child is hungry and she needs to eat!" One of them said something to the other in English. He answered okay and they, too, started to pull up carrots and cabbages until our bags were completely full. They packed all of us into the jeep and gave us a pretty long ride towards home. We found out they were stationed in the schoolhouse above the street from our apartment complex. One of them had been very outgoing and friendly, smiling almost constantly with smiling eyes, dark curly hair and a nice tan. He looked very Italian; we found this to be true after introducing himself at the end of our journey from the country.

His name was Salvadore Drago who later was to become and still is to this day, my dearest uncle. I noticed how he kept looking at my Aunt Anne Louise and smiling at her. I even saw him wink a time or two. Of course, she was a very pretty 18 year old. She was about 5 feet 8 inches with blonde shoulder-length hair, beautiful blue eyes and a shapely slender figure. She turned heads when any males passed her on the streets. I think that she liked him right away; she would smile back at him all the while blushing. He would come over whenever he could and visit with us, always bringing something for me, candy bars, chewing gum, and one day he brought me a banana. I couldn't remember ever eating one. If I did, it was a long time ago. I know that banana tasted so delicious. We all called him "Sal."

One day he came over in a big army truck and took me for a ride around the block. It was so exciting. After he dropped me off, he said he was taking the truck back and then he was coming back to talk to Mom and her sisters. I said, "Okay." I went inside and told them what he said and that he wanted to talk to them. About thirty minutes later, he rang the doorbell, came in, greeted everyone and sat down in a chair at the kitchen able. Looking pretty serious, he motioned to Mom, Aunt Erna and Aunt Anne Louise to have a seat also, and then he said, "I have a proposition for you girls." Mom and her sisters looked at each other with their eyebrows raised. Sal laughed and holding his right hand up said, "It's business." By now, they were really looking astonished and Sal started laughing. How would you like to do mine and some other GI's laundry in exchange for food? Mom and my Aunts let go a sigh of relief and told him they would love to do it. It meant we would all have food to eat in exchange for doing their laundry.

Of course, in those days there were no automatic washers and dryers. Every apartment house had a room in the basement that had an oven built out of stone and cement that was heated with wood or coal. On top was a round kettle inserted that held water. The white clothes were boiled in hot water and then removed into a wooden trunk that contained sudsy water and a wash board. After that, they were rinsed in two other tubs and wrung out before hung up on a clothes line to dry. After that procedure, they were then ironed. It was very hard work indeed, but Mom and her sisters were willing to do it. It meant having food on the table and in our bellies.

Their day would start at 4 a.m. with the fire having to be started in the brick stove to get the water heated inside the kettle. Handling those fatigues was in itself a big job and the girls often complained of their wrists hurting from ringing the water from them. All in all, it was pretty much an all day job, but the soldiers liked the way the clothes were done and kept bringing in food in exchange for their hard earned labor.

One day, they brought a whole case of cream style corn, a food that none of us had ever eaten, so we opened the cans pouring out the contents into a bowl and ate it. We had corn for breakfast, corn for lunch, corn for supper or whenever we got hungry until we all got sick of corn, even making up a little song about it.

By now, Sal came each evening to see Anne Louise and they would go out for long walks, holding hands. I sort of felt like my aunt was being taken away from me, and I started to ask if I could come along. Most of the time the answer was "NO." Of course, that would make me pout and sulk. I, too, wanted to spend time with Sal and my favorite aunt. Everyone could tell that they were in love. He brought her gifts and bouquets of wildflowers that he picked himself. Some of the bouquets came out of someone's garden; heaven only knows whose.

More and more Americans started dating German girls. They seemed to be very attracted to the blond-haired, blue-eyed Fräuleins. One such pretty blonde lived in the apartment building across the street. I would look out the window and watch her. I was fascinated by all the beautiful clothes she wore and those stiletto heels. She was a real attention getter with her tall, slender, yet very shapely body and that long shoulder-length blonde hair. She had this swivel hip walk and she was mostly accompanied by one or sometimes two GIs. They were always laughing and seemed to have a good time with each other. They usually followed her inside the building. I wondered if she, too, washed their clothes in exchange for those beautiful clothes and shoes that she wore, but she really did not look like the type that did laundry all day long. I wondered what sort of work she did - - -All the kids on the block got to talking about her and saying there goes "swivel Hips Heddy" (that was her name). A lot of the German girls that dated GIs started to wear nice clothes and those thin nylons on their legs. Those things were not available in German stores during this period. I remember wishing that I, too, could wear some of those nice clothes. Oh, I got new clothes because I was a growing child, but they were not new bought clothes from a store. They were usually cut down from some of my Mom's or Aunt's dresses. A lady that was a seamstress and lived in our same building altered dresses down to my size. I remember to this day how badly my feet would hurt being all cramped up in shoes that were too small and too tight for my feet. It left my toes not very appealing to look at. When I became older and wore sandals or cut out shoes, there was a time that one guy laughed when he looked down at my feet and said, "Your big toes look like snake heads!" I looked at him and said "Thanks!" but I felt so humiliated and hurt inside. (He later became my husband.) We just didn't have any money to buy new shoes, and the only place you could buy things was on the "Black Market."

The economy started to boom so more and more people would trade and sell all sorts of things. We had a man come to our apartment every two weeks and bring us several dozen eggs in exchange for American tobacco and cigarettes which my Mom and Aunts had earned in exchange for doing laundry for the Americans. Yes, everyone had to struggle and find a way of survival to get through these meager and tough times. More and more Americans were occupying Germany and a number of them had their families from the US join them. They were the higher ranked military personnel, such as Generals, Majors and other officers. German housing that had not been destroyed and some beautiful villas were made available for their living facilities. Their wives would ride around Nuremberg in beautiful American cars. (We called them limousines.) They were shipped from the States. They also had all the conveniences from home having the privilege of purchasing all their clothes at the BX and foods from the commissary. They had their own bowling alley on the base, a night club, snack bar and medical services.

I was so fascinated seeing all these pretty American women driving around in these street cruisers wearing all the beautiful clothes and shoes. One of my favorites was a lady who wore a beautiful red wool coat and she wore red penny loafers. I started to dream and fantasize that one day when I was all grown up, I would marry an American soldier and he would buy me a beautiful red coat and red penny loafers. After that we would go to America and live in a beautiful house with a white fence around it. I would drive a white with brown trim station wagon that would hold our six children. Yes, we would have a pair of twin boys, then a girl, then twin girls and last another boy. Oh, I had it all figured out.

Germany started making progress by rebuilding and repairing a lot of the houses and businesses, but there was still a wide shortage and several families had to share a large apartment. If it was a three bedroom, they had to share it with two other families in order for each family to have a bedroom. Everyone would have access to the kitchen and bathroom. Mom started to look for a place of our own for her sisters now all were dating and things were getting crowded. We found a large bedroom in an apartment on the third floor on the other side of town. The people who owned the apartment had a grown daughter, age 20, and there was also another lady and her little girl who rented a bedroom from them. Mom and I rented the other one. Ours was a corner room that had four large windows. Then, on each corner wall, it was heated with a pot belly stove and we had a bed, a night stand, and in the corner of the room was a round table and two chairs. A small dresser lined one of the other walls. It was our new home. All we had to move in was our few clothes and shoes and some other small items. Mom bought a two-eye burner that would add for our cooking needs or warm up soup or make tea in a pot.

CHAPTER V

OUT ON OUR OWN AGAIN

It was sort of nice, Mom and me being alone again in our own place that really belonged to someone else. We had lots more room to sleep; for this bed was much larger than the small one that we slept on for several months at my aunt's house.

Sal and Anne Louise were now engaged and they had started the paper work for plans of getting married as soon as possible. I was told that I would get to be a flower girl in their wedding; how exciting, I couldn't wait! After all, that was one big event coming up. I remembered having been a flower girl in my Aunt Erna's wedding when she got married to Uncle Otto, her second husband.

Mom was now working on the cleanup of the city, as so many others were doing. It did not pay much and it was hard work handling bricks and working with picks and shovels. She soon had to give it up as she hurt her back. She had lost so much weight and grew so thin. She really looked sick, and I was so worried about her, wishing my Dad would soon come home and help us. Food was still rationed with a small amount of sugar, milk, flour, tea and a few potatoes being handed out. Each person got one egg per week. Mom would give me a lot of her share. She would say, "You need it more than me. You are a growing child and you need to get good strong bones and healthy teeth."

It started getting colder and colder. Winter was almost upon us and that large bedroom with its four large windows was not easily heated. I remember seeing those windows covered with ice flowers from top to bottom; I couldn't even look outside. Mom bought some small pieces of wood and bark off trees for 50 pennies in order to burn them in the potbelly stove. We did not have enough money to buy coal. I stayed so cold all the time. Mom would turn on the little electric burner and hold our hands and feet over the top to get warmed up. Then, we would get into bed, cover up and snuggle close together to get warm.

It was now the winter in 1946, and as I mentioned before, it was very cold. School attendance was only half a day. I went in the mornings and came home at noon. There just were not enough schools left to occupy all the children at the same time for all day long. They were either destroyed or several were occupied by the American troops with that having been changed later. They were moved to regular sol-dier's barracks that had previously been occupied by the Germans. I so looked forward to school each morning in order to get the delicious hot cereals that were dipped out of what looked like large milk cans into our bowls. Several ladies had them lined up in the hallway and dipped them out with large ladles. One morning we got oatmeal; the next cream of wheat. One morning it was cooked rice in milk with raisins. They were all delicious and every hungry child welcomed this nourishing morning meal.

Word had it that the process was underway to bring all war criminals to trial with the trial being held at the very large "Justiz Gebaude" in Nuremberg at the Furtherstrasse. It was Nuremberg's largest courthouse. It was at that time all occupied by American troops. It had an American snack bar, commissary, BX, etc. German people were hired to work what was to be the "Famous Trials of Nuremberg." Mom got a part-time job there doing some office jobs such as filing, making copies and taking paperwork into the court-room. Her boss was a real nice Jewish man who was very compassionate and understanding about the hardships of war. As an employee for the trials, Mom got to eat along with other employees at the snack bar for free.

My mom asked her boss after she worked there a few days if he minded if I came there after school each day and ate in her place. He shook his head and said, "Oh no, you eat and your little girl can come and eat too each day." So, every time when Mom worked I got on the street car (which was running again by now) and rode to the court-house in the Fuertherstrasse where Mom waited for me and together we enjoyed a wonderful delicious lunch. I remem-ber when I bit into that white loaf bread sandwich for the first time thinking that it taste like a soft cake, unlike the dark rye bread I was raised on which was hard and chewy.

It was Christmas time again. Mom baked some star cookies and she hand knitted a new dress for my doll. I got a new scarf, gloves, cap and two pairs of socks. I also received an orange, a few apples and walnuts with all this having come from Mom. Aunt Anne Louise and Sal gave me some American candy and some coloring books with crayons. I was very happy over all my precious gifts and treasured each piece. Winter seemed long and very cold. Everyone antic-ipated spring and warmer temperatures. Aunt Anne Louise and Sal announced that their wedding was to be May 21, 1947, and before long that day was here.

I was ecstatic that I was their flower girl. Aunt Anne Louise was a beautiful bride and the ceremony took place in one of the beautiful Catholic churches that fortunately had not been destroyed during war time. Sal held both of her hands and looked deep into her eyes when he made his vows. It was plain to see how much love was between these two people. He said later that he could not imagine going back to the US without her. She was the big love of his life, and he was going to take her home to his Mama and Papa in Somerville, Massachusetts.

They moved into a small efficiency apartment after they were married to live there until July when his time was up in the military, and he was to return to the United States.

They would come and get me to stay on weekends with them at their apartment. I loved going over there. They always had such delicious things to eat, mostly great lunch-meat, sandwiches, puddings, cookies and Hershey bars. Uncle Sal was always so much fun to be around. He would turn the music on and take me by the hand and started dancing and singing at the same time.

One Sunday, we drove out to Stein to visit the famous "Faber Castell." It had an adjoining factory where the "Faber Castell pencils" were made and then shipped all over the world. The castle itself wasn't very large but very romantic and intimate, nestled in the midst of a beautiful park and pine tree forest. We walked through the park that took us to a small bridge that had no railings on either side. At one time a running stream of clear, sparkling water was running beneath of it, but at present the creek was dry. Uncle Sal, as I call him now, took me in his arms and started singing and dancing with me. Suddenly, he got too close to the bridge's edge. His next step backwards he took a tumble, falling flat on his back about 10 to 12 feet down and me on top of him. Of course, it knocked the breath out of both of us; his more than mine. We couldn't utter a word. Aunt Louise was screaming, while all along running to the side of the bridge to make her way down to the ditch "Are you alright?" but we could not answer her. Finally, Uncle Sal took some small breaths and so did I, and he was able to talk. I was getting the "go over" from head to toe to make sure that I was alright. I was. The three of us sat there for a while, trying to figure how this happened. Then, all at once, we bursted into a big laugh. This calls for ice cream at the BX, let's go. That was very fine with me. I was going to have my favorite vanilla/cherry ice cream. This would be my last weekend to spend with Uncle Sal and Aunt Anne Louise. They were getting ready to leave for the United States. I remember how sad I felt and wishing that I, too, could go. It was my most inner desire to go there someday and it became my wish for this Destination.

Right before their departure, we got the news that Anne Louise was pregnant with her first child. I felt happy but also a bit sad, thinking I wouldn't be their little girl any longer. I was reassured that I always would be very special to them. Uncle Sal said, "You're our oldest daughter," and then he gave me a big hug.

I got to go to the train station with them the day they left. I remember crying uncontrollably when the train started to pull out. My Aunt Erna tried to calm me down saying, "They will write to you and send you pictures." Aunt Anne Louise had promised that she would send me a red coat and a pair of red penny loafers when she got to the states, so I had a few good things to look forward to.

Time went on but Dad was still gone. Meanwhile, my Mom got a job in a cheese factory. I looked forward each day when she came home bringing me some kind of cheese. They were pieces that were not suitable to ship out to stores having been broken or with other malformations so employees were able to take them home for consumption.

Mom worked and I was left home by myself, or I wold go and spend the days with different ones of our relatives.

My paternal grandparents were among the ones that I spent the most time with, or I would visit Dad's only brother, Robert, and his new wife, Frieda. They had just returned from Bottrop, Germany which by then had been occupied by the Russians and therefore turned into an Eastern Sector. Robert had met her there and he actually helped her to escape to the West. They got married right away since she found out that she was expecting his child.

Their first and only child was born in Nuremberg, a little boy, and they named him Freddie. I loved visiting them and seeing the new baby. As he got older I could play with him, and I really looked forward to that.

One of my favorite places to go and spend time was at my second cousin's house, Emmi. We were both the same age. Her Dad was my Grandmother's brother, Robert Meyer. He and his wife Emma had four children; the oldest daughter being called "Erika," then came Klara, a son named Rainer and the youngest Emmi. We spent lots of time together playing and going to each other's apartment, (ours being a one room one).

Aunt Emma, as I called her, used to fix us mustard sandwiches for lunch along with some warm tea. It tasted good. It consisted of mustard, spread on rye bread, but when you are hungry and that is all there is to eat, you're glad to get it. No one could afford to choose to be picky in those days. Food was very scarce and hunger hurt; I found out at an early age.

When the weather was warm outside, we would go swimming at the Olympic Stadium. It had a great large pool, Olympic size. Fortunately, that was somehow not destroyed by the bombings. Emmi's sister Klara would accompany us and keep an eye on us two younger girls. It was always very exciting and so much fun to go swimming, my favorite thing to indulge in come summertime. On one such day the weather turned cloudy, and before we knew it there came a downpour of rain. Everyone ran to the dressing rooms and shelters for cover. I suddenly remembered that I had left all four of our long windows open before I left the apartment. We did this all of the time when the weather was nice in order to have fresh air in our room. I looked at Klara and Emmi and held my hand over my mouth. My eyes turned out big. I must have looked very scary when they asked me what was wrong. I said, "Oh, it is just awful. Everything will be soaked." "What will be soaked?' Klara asked. I said, ""Our apartment. My Mom will be so upset with me. "Well don't worry. It is just water and we will help you clean up." After the rain stopped we put our clothes on and headed by streetcar to our apartment building. We made our way up to the third floor gasping, and I could feel my stomach turning into knots. We walked down the hallway to our apartment building and saw that the door was already open. Mom had gotten there before we did and was already cleaning up the water that seemed to be everywhere for the wind had really blown hard and had gotten everything wet inside. The girls and I started to help but Mom sent Klara and Emmi home. She told them that we had it under control. Oh, oh, I thought. Now she is going to let me have it. Oh yes, and fussed at, I was. I was told to sit in a chair and that I would be grounded for a whole week, which meant, of course, that I had to stay in that one room all week long and could not go or visit anyone. I thought, well, I will just have to stay home and do lots of reading.

CHAPTER VI

AN AFFAIR GOING ON?

The effects of war, the daily stress of worry to have enough food for herself and her child seemed to have taken its toll on Mom's nerves, plus not hearing from my Dad and wondering if he was still alive. It seemed that the load she was carrying around was getting to be too much for her to handle at times. She became very impatient with me, like if I needed help with homework during those first few years of school. Math seemed to be a weak subject for me. Everything else was fine. I never failed it but I never got any "1s" which that was compared to an "A" here in this country. Sometimes she yelled at me and said things that Moms should not say to her child. Her temper just seemed to flare up over any little thing. She was arguing with her sisters and brother. She was getting very moody and sort of restless. Thus, that behavior of hers made me very nervous, and I started the habit of blinking with my eyes, another thing I was gotten on to about for doing. Then, she would be changing over into instant nice Mom, and we would sing and laugh. She tried to teach me to sing harmony when she sang a song. She had quite a nice voice, so did all of her sisters. Sometimes when they got altogether, they would sing all kinds of German folk songs and seemed to enjoy themselves doing it. I loved listening to them.

A new lady moved into an apartment above ours. She was a war widow and was about 36 years old, quite attractive with long, auburn hair and sparkling blue eyes. Her name was Annemarie. She and Mom got to be friends. We started to visit her at her place. She got the whole apartment by herself. By then, people were moving into places that had been rebuilt. Mom and I could not afford it, so we stayed in that one room. Ms. Annemarie, as I called her, had quite a showplace. Gorgeous furniture, beautifully decorated, and she wore beautiful clothes as well. One evening, as we visited, we got to meet her GI boyfriend. He just showed up. They kissed at the door as she led him in and just nonchalantly introduced him as Joe. Of course, Mom and I left. However, this GI Joe thought my Mom was a very pretty young woman, which she was, and about ten years younger than Annemarie. He also had a friend, that I did not meet until later, but Mom started going out some at night. She really did not tell me precisely where she was going or who with. I started to spend quite a few nights with different relatives and some weekends. They included my Gussmann grandparents, Aunt Frieda and Uncle Robert, Aunt Erna (Mom's sister), and even a great aunt, Aunt Binner.

Looking back now, it reminded my life of that one of a traveling little Gypsy. Mom would tell me that her and Annemarie went to movies and visited other friends which they had in common. (I did not know any of them.)

One day Mom and I walked downtown Nuremberg when we ran into my maternal grandfather, George Friedrich. I really never knew him very well. He soon remarried after my grandmother died at the young age of 45 and fathered another child, a boy named Peter. He was close to my age, very cute, and when he grew up to be a young man he could have passed for a Tom Selleck double, a very handsome young man. He turned heads whenever he was around ladies of all ages. Anyway, I do not remember ever sitting on my grandfather's lap and him telling me a story nor giving me a hug. Maybe he did years ago when I was small and my grandmother was still alive. So, we just stood there and talked to him for about ten minutes. Then, he was on his merry way. Bye grandpa.

When Aunt Anne Louise and Uncle Sal married, little Peter was the ring carrier in Aunt Anne Louise and Uncle Sal's wedding, and I was the little flower girl. I still have that picture.

I was getting mail from Aunt Anne Louise and Uncle Sal now and then. They lived I Somerville, Massachusetts. The last letter included a couple of pictures – one of Aunt Anne Louise right before her first baby was due. The other one was of their new daughter Rita. She was precious and very beautiful with head full of dark hair and dimples in her cheeks. For some strange reason I felt a bit jealous and felt like someone had taken my place away from my favorite aunt and uncle. I think they suspected how I would feel because at the end of the letter, my uncle wrote "Remember, Helga, you are now our oldest daughter and we still love you." That made me feel much better. I showed Mom the letter and pictures. Sighing, I made the comment, "Gosh, I wish I was in America and could see all three of them. I would love to hold their new baby." Mom just shook her head at me and said, "You and longing to go to America all of the time. Maybe someday you will get to go." My thought to myself was "I know I will."

The city of Nuremberg was now in a huge process of being rebuilt. Construction sites were going on everywhere and many jobs were created for people who did not have any. Of course, it would take quite some time to have the city rebuilt as it once was before the demolition of all the severe bombings. Some of the medieval structures that were destroyed were trying to be reconstructed as closely to its originality as possible.

It is now autumn of 1947 and I miss my Dad terribly. Life seems so much emptier without him, and my favorite aunt and uncle having moved away overseas. Time was nearing Christmas. We have not heard from him except we knew now that he was a "prisoner of war" kept somewhere in a prison camp in France.

Mom was knitting every evening, especially after I went to bed. She did not want me to see what she was making. She started baking a few sugar cookies and I drew stars and moons, colored and cut them out for Christmas ornaments to hang on our tree. Our tree was not very large, but it was real and smelled wonderful of wintergreen. We had clip on candles that were lit for the first time on Christmas Eve. That was when we celebrated Christmas. After the tree was lit, I got to come back into the room (after having to stay out in the hallway. There was not another room to go into). Then, I heard this horn blowing. As I entered the room the window was open and Mom said the Christ Child had come to bring me presents. She then closed the window, making me think that the Christ Child had exited through there. So, then I saw my presents. My old doll got a new beautifully knitted dress that she had made. She made me a new cap, gloves, scarf and two new pairs of socks – all the usual. I also got some apples, an orange and walnuts. The tree was beautiful with its silver icicles hanging down and all of the real candles burning. Mom and I sang Silent Night, Holy Night. Then we ate spice cookies and drank our spice tea. A little later we attended midnight mass. The snow had started falling as we exited the church and it was very cold, but it was so beautiful.

Christmas Day we visited Mom's family and we also went by my paternal grandparents, the Gussmann's house. I received some small gifts from all of them. They were nothing of great value but given with love, and every little thing in those days meant so much to me.

The month of January was now upon us and it was very cold. I only had school in the mornings. Classes were held in shifts as there was still a shortage of school houses and also teachers. I got home in time for lunch. Mom would usually have a bowl of soup, stew or something warm for me to eat. Hot tea was very welcomed. Ice flowers decorated all four of our windows in the large room which could not be very well heated from burning tree barks in the small pot belly stove. The other heating unit we had was that two-eye electric burner on which our food was warmed – and our feet and hands. Yes, it served for that as well. Afterward, Mom and I crawled into bed and we took a nap, mainly to get warm, a thing that became a daily habit.

I started to pick up bits and pieces from my relatives when they had conversations and they thought I was not listening, but I did listen. I seemed to always be very mature for a child my age. Talk was that Mom was seeing an American GI by the name of Paul. Other things were said, such as what will my Dad do if and when he returns home and finds out. This really upset me. I loved my Dad and missed him with all of my heart. I could not talk to anyone about it, but I cried every night in bed when no one could see or hear me and I prayed "Please dear God, send my Daddy home soon."

I finally met Paul one day. Mom said he was just a good friend. He was very nice looking, tall, dark complected, black hair and dark eyes. He had those thick, long eye lashes. He was very nice to me and gave me some American chocolate. Then, he invited Mom and me to the snack bar on base for ice cream. I loved ice cream and hardly ever got any, especially none as good as the American one during that time. Paul said he was from San Francisco and that he would like to take me and Mom back to the states. That was one time that I did not like to hear about going to the states. Oh no, I cannot leave my Daddy. Paul just smiled and exposed two rows of perfect white teeth. Gosh, he was really good looking, but not as good looking as my Dad by no means. I found out (from relatives' conversations and me ears dropping) that Paul was in love with my mother and wanted to marry her. Also, that he was very jealous of her and could not stand to see another man look at her. All of this upset me terribly and my eyelids were blinking like crazy once more. I could not understand what had gotten in to my Mom. How could she date another man when my Dad might come home any day? I think she was angry that the war was over for quite some time now and other men had come home to their families and she was still alone to struggle by herself. So, she sort of reached to another man for support and have someone to lean on, but my Dad could not help it being gone. He was kept a prisoner of war as we learned later. Of course, when he finally communicated with his family, at that time he did not even know where Mom and I lived, so he contacted his parents. He let them know that he might be released soon, but they did not have much contact with Mom during that time because of her having an affair. So, they just dropped a few hints to him that he might find some surprises about Mom when he got home. Therefore, he never contacted us. I found this out later when I was grown up and Dad told me how hurt he was, but he did not want to leave her because of me.

Looking back now, I don't hold it against my Mom for what she did. None of us are perfect nor without flaw. Mom was a very young woman with a heavy load on her young shoulders. She was lonesome and just needed someone to hold her and talk to. I don't believe that she ever loved another man at that time. She just missed Dad terribly and did not know if he would ever return. Paul soon learned that Mom was not about to divorce my Dad and go with him to the states. His time, however, was up and he had to leave. He told her if she ever changed her mind he would come to get her and me. I knew in my heart it would not be me going. I would definitely stay with my Dad.

CHAPTER VII

A LATE CHRISTMAS HOMECOMING

Today is January 19, 1948. Mom said "Do you know what today is?" I looked at her, shaking my head. She said "Today is mine and your Dad's anniversary. It would be nice if Dad was here," she said. "I know," I replied. We ate our meager lunch and then laid down for our daily nap. It was another bitter, cold day. The ice flowers sparkled like silver on the windows. They were pretty to look at, but it was so uncomfortable looking at them and being so cold. I looked over at Mom. She had already fallen asleep. Suddenly, I heard the doorbell, ring, ring, ring. That was three times, our ring. The shield by the main entrance had three name tags. The people who owned that apartment had one ring. The other lady and her little girl that also rented a room, theirs was two times, ours, Gussmann: three times. There it was again, ring, ring, ring. Mom did not hear it and I did not want to wake her up, so I slipped out of bed and tiptoed over to the door. I opened it and walked down the long hallway towards the front door of the apartment. The upper part of the door was made of glass covered by a lace curtain. I could see the shape of a man standing outside. I carefully opened the crack of the door and peeked out at this strangely dressed man. He wore what looked like an old soldier's cap. His upper body was covered with a heavy top coat that had the letters "P.W." painted on it. (At that time I had no idea what that stood for.) One of his pant legs had a hole in it exposing part of his knee, and his shoes were made of wood that you just slip into. I learned later that in France they called them "sabbots." The man's face looked thin and pale. He had a thin mustache and beautiful deep blue eyes that looked very curiously at me, as curiously as I looked at him. I thought that he was very handsome. Then I asked him what he wished. Hesitantly, he asked if this was Gussmann's residence. I said that it was, and then I noticed large tears swelling up in his eyes as he said with a very shaky voice, "Helga?" At that moment I thought my little heart was going to jump out of my chest as I, too, started crying, calling out "Daddy, Daddy," throwing myself into his arms. He picked me up, hugging me closely as he made his way into the hallway pulling the door shut behind him.

We walked towards our one-room home. As he entered the room, still carrying me, I cried "Mom, wake up, wake up, Daddy's home!" Dad and I both were crying and laughing all at the same time. Mom finally sat up in bed looking very confused. She thought that either she or I was having a nightmare, but finally she realized the picture in front of her was real, so she got up and made her way towards us. The three of us just hugged and cried. It was the most relieved feeling I have ever experienced in my young life. I knew that everything would be alright from now on. Daddy was here and he would take care of us and everything else. I knew after listening to some of their conversation that they had a lot of things to talk about and to work out. I knew one thing for sure. I would not let go of my Daddy ever again. The next morning Dad went to school with me.

Holding a smiling little girl by the hand, he met my teacher. She was happy to meet him and told him how glad she was that he was finally home. She told him how I always talked about him and wishing for his return. Dad replied that he was very happy to be back home, also. Then, he asked her if he could keep me out of school for the day. Smiling, and with tears in her eyes, she said, "Mr. Gussmann, you keep your little girl home the rest of this week. She will catch up on what she has to miss." Wow, I did not expect that. I was so happy. I would spend all day with my Dad and the next and the next. We had so many relatives to visit and everyone was so happy. It truly was a wonderful occasion and a very happy time for me.

Even though this was a very happy time for me to have my Dad back in my life, the relationship between him and my Mom had grown very strained and rather cold. There were many questions unresolved between the two of them. My Dad was not staying with us at night. He slept at my grandparents' place. On weekends, I stayed there also, but I had to stay with Mom on weekdays because of school. After a couple of weeks Dad got an apartment that was easy for him to obtain since he had been a prisoner of war. He was also hired on as a demolition expert, a very dangerous job indeed. He was hired as foreman and had a crew of ten men. They had to dig up bombs that had been dropped but never went off. Some were buried in the ground after they were extracted. All of his men cleared the site and then my Dad went on to dismantle the bomb. There were about three or four experts with each having their own crews. Mom was tired of living with other tenants in one room, so after her and Dad talked a lot and things seemed to be going better between them, she decided to move in with Dad, a dream come true for me. I wanted things to be good between them and for us to be a real family again. I had to change over to a new school and make all new friends, but I really did not mind that at all. I took it on as a challenge. At least it meant now I, too, have a Dad I would talk about to my friends and teachers and who would help me with my homework.

Dad would catch a train every morning to head to the main office that was located in Feucht. From there, they were sent on to different locations. Mom, too, got a new job at the Wicklein Cookie Factory. They made the famous, world known, "Nurnberger Lebkuchen." Life seemed to be going pretty well by now. Food supplies were plentiful. We did not have to go too hungry any more. On weekends we would go for walks if the weather was permitting and not too cold. We would usually meet up with my grandparents and other friends, heading toward the outskirts of Nuremberg and took walks into the beautiful pine forests. In the summer months there were plenty of blueberries and mushrooms which we all picked and carried back home with us. Mom used to fix those little yellow mushrooms into some sort of sauce and serve them over boiled potatoes and a vegetable on the side, and that was one of our favorite meals. The blueberries we ate fresh and used them to eat along with pancakes. If we had lots of them and Mom had plenty of sugar, she made blueberry jam, so we would enjoy that in the winter months.

My first Holy Communion was coming up, but I had no dress, shoes nor any of the rest of the apparel that was needed for this beautiful sacrament celebration. The Black Trading Market was going in full gear. People were trading all sorts of things, food, clothing, household items, etc. One day my Dad came home carrying an American parachute. I have to chuckle thinking about some American soldier jumping out of a plane and his parachute was turned into my first Holy Communion dress, but that is exactly what happened. Our friend who was also a seamstress did quite a good job making a real pretty white dress. It had long sleeves and a ruffle was added around the bottom. I certainly thought that it was very pretty. My white linen shoes were also a trade project. My floral wreath for my hair, my white stockings, prayer book and candle was furnished by the Nuns from our Catholic Church. I was so proud to wear my new watch that my Dad had brought back from France for which he had to work many hours as a farmhand while he was a French prisoner of war. All of our relatives were invited for this beautiful celebration. I even had a cake. It was a great day and I felt so beautiful inside and out in my beautiful dress made from an American parachute.

Life went on. My parents both worked and I went to school. I lived happy and secure having gained back a normal family life. On one of the evenings when my Dad returned from work, he seemed real depressed and his facial color was extra pale. Mom and I both asked him was he okay or was he sick, but he just dropped his head, wiping a tear from his eye. He started to tell us about the tragedy that had happened that day. One of Dad's best friends, a fellow demolition expert, was killed that day. It blew him to bits. While trying to dismantle a bomb, somehow he had touched the wrong wire and that was it. It was a horrible thing to have happened. We all felt so bad thinking about what his poor family must be going through. It made Mom and me both realize how dangerous a job Dad must be performing every day, and it hit us with bare realization. He needs to quit doing this. Sure, he was making very good money, but all of the money in the world would not be worth him losing his own life over. From then on, if his train happened to be late getting in or Dad stopped somewhere or ran in to someone and talked awhile before coming home, Mom and I were nervous and started looking out of the window and pacing the floor. So, things became strained again. Mom was always uneasy. I was scared and fearful that something bad was going to happen to my Dad.

CHAPTER VIII

BACK TO FRANCE

One evening after we ate dinner and the three of us were still sitting at the table sipping our tea, Dad looked at Mom and me and said, "I think the three of us need a big change and get away and out of this still demolished city, stay gone a few years until everything has been rebuilt and then come back." He went on to say "You know, I have a lot of experience in farm work and I think it would be good for us to live on a farm for a while, so how would you two like to go to France and live there for a few years? I hear they are in need of help on farms and it doesn't pay too badly either." Mom and I just stared at him. We could not believe what we were hearing. Then, Mom said "You just got back from there where you were held a prisoner of war!" He laughed and said "Well, I will not be a prisoner when I go back on my own free will. Besides, I will have you two with me and we can live a good, clean and healthy life. You and Helga can live in another country and learn to speak French, he said. France is very pretty, especially in the countryside.

Well, I sort of got excited then, the idea of moving to a new country, especially one where my Dad had been held prisoner of war for three and a half years. Anyway, Dad said it would only be for a while until things became better here and then we would move back. So, we agreed and we started making arrangements to move to France. Of course, there was lots of paperwork involved – passports, working permits for both of my parents and a new place to live, which turned out to be an estate that hired both of my parents.

Now, my grandparents and other relatives and friends were dismayed about our decision. They did not like seeing my Dad and us leaving again so soon after having just returned not too long ago from being kept a P.O.W. My grandparents were also upset about losing their only granddaughter, besides their son. (I happened to be my grandpa's Apple of the Eye.) They would have to be content just having little Freddy around, my Uncle Robert and Aunt Frieda's only child. We sold what little furniture we owned and packed our clothes, shoes, working utensils, along with towels and linens. They were shipped ahead to our new address Epensival sur Epense sur Marne in France. After several emotional goodbyes with family and friends, we left Nuremberg in the early part of September 1949 and headed by train towards our new neighboring country, France.

We arrived in Nancy as it started to get dark. The train that we were supposed to take to Chalons sur Marne did not have a connection. Everyone seemed upset and the question surfaced as to where we would spend the night. After several discussions with authorities, we were told that there were several homes and nearby farms that were willing to take us in for the night.

By then, nightfall was here. We took a ride on the shuttle bus that would take us to our destination. Ours was a nearby farmhouse. The room that was made available to us – a true "nightmare" I have never forgotten, and until this day has inflicted a horrible fear in me towards mice and rats. The room only had one double bed, a chair, and a washstand. It was very old and uncomfortable. Mice and rats seemed to live there. After checking the bed really well, Mom and I got in it, but my Dad sat in the nearby chair all night to make sure no mice or rats would get on the bed. I was horrified and cried myself to sleep clinging close to my Mom.

Early the next morning we were offered some white French bread, coffee and milk which we all welcomed, for we were really hungry by then. Shortly thereafter, we joined others who were already seated on the bus that picked us up and carried us to the train station where we were to resume our trip to Chalons sur Marne.

We arrived sometime after noon. We were told to go to a large room in order to meet our new Patron, Monsieur Andre Guillaume, who also had an older brother Ghislain. They were both proprietors of Epensival. Their wives, Denise and Marie, were in charge of running the large house and the domestic help. So, after being introduced, we got in a very nice car and started towards Epensival. We had to go through Epense which had a distance between the two of them of about two kilometers. Epense was a customary French village consisting of a Mayor's office, a school house, a small post office, a pub, and a couple of stores beside, also church and residential homes. It was very picturesque, especially the drive to Epensival with its large shade trees on each side of the road. Beyond the rows of trees lay fields of wheat, oats, potatoes and other products that grew there. The estate was visible from a distance, a very old structure that dated back to the time of Napoleon Bonaparte who, by the way, it was told had spent one night in Epensival on one of his travels through France.

The color of the house was a chalk white. It was two stories high with bedrooms on the second floor that had large balconies leading to the outside and a beautiful view of the estate. Downstairs was a large façade of stone, a huge entrance and very long windows. It looked like a small castle. Inside was a large dining room on one side leading into a huge kitchen. On the opposite side was a large living room with an adjoining music room, a library with office and another sitting room they called the "Ladies Tea Room." I was fascinated. Monsieur Ghislain and his wife Marie did not have any children. Madame Denise and Monsieur Antoine had an 8-month-old little boy. I could tell right away they all seemed to be taking a big liking towards me, especially Monsieur Ghislain. He always smiled. We were told that they came originally from Belgium when they bought Epensival. He and his wife loved children but remained childless.

There were three other small houses on the estate. We got to live in one of them and it was really nice. I even had my own bedroom; something I hadn't had since we were bombed out.

I was admitted into the local School of Epense. One large room held grades 1 – 8. After that, they had to go to Givry on Argonne. I really felt anxious when my Dad walked me to the school the next day. Of course, he could speak the language. I didn't have a clue. I left Germany when I was in the third grade. Now, I was to start the fourth, so the teacher handed me a French-German dictionary and a first grade reader and said to me "learn French." Hmm - - I thought. I have my job cut out. But, as it turned out, I really learned very fast, but not from the dictionary or the first grade reader. No, I learned from the French children and I learned to say "quest ce que c'est" (What is this?) and they would tell me, and I would repeat and remember. Pretty soon, I could pretty well converse with my new friends.

When the weather was nice, I walked to and from school. When it was rainy or really cold, I got a ride from one of the "Patrons." I got to have a dog named "Bijou" a beagle hound. She was a puppy that Monsieur Ghislain gave me when his dog had little ones. I had never owned a dog and I loved my new friend. Monsieur Ghislain would go rabbit hunting in the woods behind the estate and sometimes he would give us one of the rabbits that he killed, and Mom fixed a nice dinner of sweet and sour rabbit with potato balls. It really tasted good!

The forest behind the estate had the most beautiful flowers growing in it. I remember picking lots of violets and Lily of the Valley. I used to keep a vase on my night table in my room and the whole room smelled wonderful. Monsieur Ghislain and his wife Marie used to take me to town with them on Saturdays, and we would visit some of the French pastry shops and eat those wonderful Eclairs and other delicious desserts.

We kept real close contact with our families in Germany and my Grandmother would send me German children's books to read. She said she did not want me to forget my "mother language." I told her in a letter – "Never."

I got along great with most of the French children, except for a few. They were "German haters" due to all of the war crimes that had happened. Of course, they didn't stop to think that I, too, had suffered tremendously and had lost a lot. None of it was my fault, yet some of them gave me mean looks and made hateful comments, even the teacher I had was not very nice to me. He was a tall, thin man with natural wavy hair and he wore big black horn-rimmed glasses. He used to be really firm with me and never gave me a smile. One day during class I let out a giggle because one of the children had said something really funny which made me laugh. So, he called me up front and started yelling at me using some words of me being a no good German pig. Then, he told me to turn around and go back to my desk. When I turned to walk off, he started kicking me in the rear end with his foot several times following me to where my desk was. I started crying and ran all of the way to the door of the classroom which was located in the center of the back of the room. I opened the door and kept on running all of the way to Epensival, crying the whole time. When I got to the estate, I saw my Dad talking to Monsieur Ghislain. They both looked startled when they saw me, and I still cried so hard that I could hardly talk. Finally, after my Dad held me and calmed me down, I told them what happened. Monsieur Ghislain said "Come on Hans and bring Helga with you. We are going to Epense." He got his car out of the garage and picked us up. My Dad's face was pale and his jaws were clenched together. Monsieur Ghislain said "Don't worry Hans. I will take care of this matter." We drove straight to the Mayor's office, went inside, and after exchanging a few words with the Mayor, they had me to tell again what happened. Then they talked some more and we went home. I did not go back to school the next day or the next. Then there was the weekend. When my Dad reassured me that it was okay to go back, I did. To my surprise, there was a new teacher. A beautiful, young, dark-haired, French woman with the prettiest blue eyes and a nice smile. She said "Hello Helga." I never saw that mean man again. I really don't know what happened to him. What's more, I didn't want to know.

We took several interesting trips, especially school trips which included the city of Reims where we visited the Cathedral and the world famous "Champagne Caves." They even let us taste some of the champagne, but just a little, not too much. France has lots of old castles and they are nestled here and there and all are medieval. I always found the countryside to be very picturesque. By now, I spoke French pretty well and I did a lot of Mom's grocery shopping with her as I could read and tell her what it said. My Dad worked really hard, but it seemed to be very becoming to his looks. He had a good suntan and looked healthy. He did a bit of everything. He milked cows, worked in the fields, and he and Mom seemed to have worked out all of their personal problems, so maybe this move to France was good for all of us after all.

Mom worked mostly in the main house with house chores and helped with preparing some of the meals, but I remember when the time came to harvest beets and potatoes she worked in the fields along with my Dad and other farm hands. One thing was certain, we all had plenty of food, and I started to gain weight. My parents both owned and rode bicycles. My Dad knew a man in Epense who had a nice used bike. The man told him that he could have it for me to ride. I was thrilled. Now I could ride my bike to school and back home. On weekends, we used to ride our bikes and visit other German people that were friends of ours that lived in and worked in some of the neighboring villages. Some of them had children close to my age and we used to play outdoors or play some sort of table games if the weather was permissible. Life seemed pretty good, and we were all eating well and enjoyed good health.

Monsieur Ghislain and Madame Marie had really taken an affectionate liking towards me, always giving me some sort of treat or small gift such as candy, cookies and maybe even a small toy now and then. I, too, had become very fond of them.

Right before viewing the Estate of Epensival on the way from Epense, there was a sharp curve, then it went downhill. I loved coming to that spot on my bike. I would hold both of my legs straight out and let it roll downhill. It made my adrenaline rise. Until, one day this bunny rabbit came across my bike's path. I started to swerve and finally lost total control and what a bad fall I took. Both my arms, hands and legs were skinned. I had bruises pretty much all over. I lay there in my misery and cried until I finally got myself up and hobbled over to inspect my bike. The handle bar was all bent, so were some of the spikes on my front wheel. I started pushing it towards the house. Mom was just walking from the main house towards ours when she saw me. I was still crying and sobbing. Well, I think the idea of my bike getting tore up hurt more than all the scratches and bruises. She took me inside and started cleaning my wounds and applying antiseptic ointment, Band-Aids and even bandages to some of the places. She told me Dad could probably fix my bike to where I would be able to ride it again. That he did, except the front wheel had to be replaced. I was pretty sore all over and received lots of attention from everyone the next few days.

CHAPTER IX

A TRAGEDY

One morning in early fall, I left on my bike to head to school. Mr. Ghislain waved at me and gave me his big smile as he headed towards his workshop in which he loved to work and make things out of wood. He had all sorts of tools including an electric table saw. I waved back at him as I said "Aurevoir Monsieur Ghislain." That was the last time ever saw him alive.

My Dad came to school around noon and after exchanging a few words he told me to get my things, that I was to go home early. He didn't tell me at the time what had happened. His reason for picking me up early was because he didn't want me to hear from someone else what had happened to Mr. Ghislain, as he explained to me later. My Dad's face was very solemn as we rode our bikes towards Epensival. Then after we parked them in their regular places we went upstairs to our side of the house in which we lived. I had some very uneasy feelings. Mom was sitting at the kitchen table and I could tell by looking at her eyes that she had been crying. Dad told me to have a seat as he sat down himself. Then, he took both of my hands in his and looking very sadly into my eyes said: "Honey, something terrible has happened to Monsieur Ghislain today. His brother Antoine found him in his workshop where he fell into the electric saw while it was still running. It had cut deep into his forehead. They didn't know whether he suffered a stroke or had heart attack, but it was one of the two, and while working at the electric saw he just fell over into it. There was nothing anyone could do." He went on to say that I needed to be strong and pray for his family, as I sat sobbing endlessly. I couldn't believe that my dearest friend, Mr. Ghislain, was now gone. I also immediately thought of Madame Marie and how awful she must feel with him gone as they didn't ever have any children. I did get to go over to the estate home and gave my condolences to Madame Marie, Antoine and Denise along with my parents and other farmhands.

Some of the relatives started coming in – nieces, nephews, sisters and other family members. They all stayed at the estate home as it had numerous bedrooms. Everyone attended the funeral service. It was held in the Catholic local church and then the body was moved to his final resting place. It was very, very sad and it seemed to change everything in Espensival. Madame Marie went back to live in Belgium. Antoine and Denise were now in total charge of the estate. Antoine was the opposite of his brother Ghislain, very serious. He didn't have much to say. When one spoke to him he only nodded shortly and hardly ever smiled. It changed things for everyone that was employed there, one after another started to leave.

My parents also moved to a village called Cernon s/ coole and Dad was hired by a Madame Irene Garnier to run her farm and Mom was to help her with household chores. Mme Irene was a plump and jolly little woman that always smiled, and she would chuckle at times that made her belly jump up and down. Mr. Garnier was in real bad health and unable to do any kind of physical work anymore. He was either sitting in an easy chair or lying in his bed. Mme Irene was a wonderful cook and she really introduced us to the real French cuisine. She made the best French fries I had ever tasted, and she knew how to cook a very tasty steak along with all the other delicious side dishes. The Garniers also had a large house, of which they let us occupy one side of it. I remember there was a large bedroom in which my parents slept and it had a beautiful fireplace in it. Whenever I was sick and had to stay out of school, I lay in their bed and watched the cozy fire burning. Mom would make hot tea or lemonade for me. I almost dreaded getting well. It was especially nice when it was really cold outside and snow was falling.

Right across the street from where we lived was a Catholic church. My parents and I attended Mass there on Sundays, and my school and I attended Mass on Mondays, Wednesdays and Fridays during the week. Then once a week after school we had choir practice. By now my French was fluent and I had no problems keeping up in school. My favorite subject was French history and what a beautiful history it was. I loved the history of "Jeanne d Arc." It was such a beautiful story, but had such a sad and horrendous ending. I admired her courage and her heart that so loved God and her country for which she was willing to do die for.

Mom started her rabbit breeding and selling business. It was hilarious. We had all these cages with rabbits in them. Whenever they got large enough, she sold them to a vendor that came once a week. He pulled up in his truck in front of the houses and people came out. They bought groceries, traded chickens and rabbits. He sold sugar, coffee, sausage called boudin, and all sorts of other things. My Mom by now, too, could speak a little French, but she would get things mixed up. For instance, on one of the days when several French women gathered around the peddle truck to do their shopping, Mom was also in the midst, and when it was her turn, the man asked her what she needed. She told him some sugar and coffee, then she blurted out and one pound of "putain." The man's eyes widened and he started to laugh out loud as the other women who also heard her comment were laughing as well. Putting both hands on his hips and looking at Mom, still laughing, he exclaimed "Sorry, but I don't have any "Putain" for sale. Mom shouted "oui, oui" and pointed to a ring of sausage that lay over by a shelf. He said "oh, c'est boudin," so what she had asked for instead of a pound of sausage was a pound of whore. After he explained it all to her, she was so embarrassed but they all just laughed. They knew that she couldn't speak the language very well.

I didn't have any more trouble with teachers or children while going to school. As a matter of fact, I made friends wherever I went. We were still in constant contact with our relatives in Germany. They missed us and we missed them. We were told that the economy was on the rise and Nuremberg along with other heavily demolished cities in Germany was rapidly being rebuilt. We knew and we talked about lots of times that we would be going back home in the near future, but, for now, Mom and Dad would keep working until they had enough money saved up to get a nice new apartment and all new furniture whenever we were ready to make our move.

Lots of times in the afternoons when I got out of school, I used to go to the milking stable where my Dad milked the cows, a job he performed by hand mornings and evenings every day. I can still see him now, sitting on a three legged wooden stool and wearing a French beret on his head, just milking away. He milked the milk into a bucket which was then emptied into large milk cans. Sometimes when I was not looking he would squirt some of the milk at me. Then I ran out in a hurry, hearing him laugh behind me.

My Dad heard from a friend who used to work with him that they were hiring mechanics and machinists in a factory called Labesse located in Sezanne sur Marne. Dad decided to look into it. He caught a train carrying his bike along. It would be nice if he could get hired on. It would mean lots more money than his earnings on a farm. When the personnel officials saw my Dad's previous training credentials which he had obtained in the military and also previously as a civilian, they hired him immediately in maintenance to repair their machinery and whatever else needed to be repaired. Upon his return, he discussed it with Mom. Then, he gave a 2-week notice to Mme Irene, who hated to lose us. She was crying and hugging us and told us we could home back anytime. We told her that we would miss her also.

Dad had found a real small apartment for us in Sezanne. It was on the second floor. The kitchen was really small, you couldn't pass each other at the same time, then a living room and very small bedroom, so Mom and Dad decided they would use the living room for their bedroom and I could use the small bedroom. It had to do for now until we found something larger. This was our first time living inside a small city since we left Germany. It had its good parts about it. There were all kinds of stores in walking distance; so was the school I was to attend. Sezanne was a very old and charming small town. I am sure by now it has grown into a large city as have many others all over the world as well. Dad seemed to like his new job but more so liked the better wages. It wasn't long until my Mom was also hired at the factory for the production line. I loved my new teacher Madame Nonotiere. She seemed to have taken a big liking to me. She loved oranges and ate 3 or 4 of them every day while she was teaching class. Mardi Gras was here and I got to dress up in a long dress and would walk with the other children in the parade through the city. I was so thrilled to be a part of it. Mom and Dad watched me from the sideline. They clapped and waved at me. I felt so proud being in that parade.

We had always wanted to visit the wonderful city of Paris. So, one long weekend we did just that. We stayed at a small hotel on one of the side streets close to the Mont Martre. It wasn't anything fancy, just cheap and clean. After all, we came to do some sightseeing, not to spend time in some fancy hotel. We walked through Mont Martre. I was astonished to see all the Parisian street artists at work and the beautiful art work some of them performed. I just stood and watched them painting on their canvases. We walked down the Champs Elisees, Arc the Triumph, visited the beautiful medieval Notre Dame Cathedral and visited the first and second Stage of the famous Eiffel Tower. What a beautiful city it is indeed and I just went Ah and Oh at the way the Paris people dressed. I had never seen so many beautiful dressed up women. There were quite a few Americans that visited Paris, also. To me, they always stood out. I could spot them anywhere. I still loved the Americans and loved watching hem driving their colorful limousines around town. Getting back to Paris, we ate at some sidewalk cafes and the food was "magnifique" as the French would say. How fun to sit and eat great food and at the same time watching people passing by.

By now, we had adopted a lot of the French customs and also cooked some French cuisine which was very tasty. I loved the French bread called baguette The French people had a habit to carry the baguettes under their arm and while walking at a fast pace they would break off pieces and eat while walking down the street, a habit that I, too, enjoyed and copied and made use of whenever my Mom would send me to the bakery. Of course, when I arrived back home with my baguette, Mom always said, "I believe a mouse got hold of this bread!" I loved the French National Holiday called "Bastille Day" celebrated on July 14th. It is like the 4th of July in the states. The French really celebrate on this occasion with lots of music, wine and dancing in the streets. There were also fairs and lots of amusements for adults and children of all ages.

Spring of 1951, I was now 12 years old and we moved to the outskirts of Sezanne, close to where the factory was located that employed my parents. The place that we moved into had actually been built to use as a large garage. It had windows and a large wooden slide door for an opening. The floor was a slick finished concrete that was constantly moped by me or my Mom. My Dad put up walls with the help of a couple of his friends and divided it up into two bedrooms, a very large kitchen-dining room and a very small bathroom sink and toilet only. We had to take sponge baths on weekdays and on weekends we had a large galvanized tub that was filled with water heated on top of the stove. Mom and Dad took their baths on Friday nights; I had mine on Saturday.

I rode my bike to school. It was still the same old one that I had in Epensival. I also would ride down the road to a farm and pick up eggs in a basket for my Mom. She always baked some kind of good cake for the weekend. When I was out of school and my parents worked, I had chores to do at the house – make up beds, clean and put on supper, mostly potato soup for which I had to peel the potatoes and cut them into cubes, then leave them set in water with salt until Mom finished cooking the soup after she got home.

CHAPTER X

BACK HOME FOR A VISIT

My grandparents really missed me and wanted me to come home during summer vacation. So, Mom and Dad told me that I would go for one month. I was so excited. We knew another German couple. They were from Ansbach which is not too far from Nuremberg. They were returning back home and they said that they would keep an eye on me until they got off. My Grandfather was to pick me up at the train station in Nuremberg. The days previous for my departure were very anxious and exciting. We had to pack my suitcase that would hold enough clothes for several changes so that my grandmother would not have to do a lot of extra laundry, but there was also a bit of sadness in me, thinking I would not get to see my parents for a whole month. Well, but then I thought about how long it had been since I got to hug my Grandpa and Grandma and that gave me the go ahead. I kissed and hugged my parents goodbye. Then, my Dad put me and my suitcase on the train. The conductor was to keep an eye on me as well. The young couple that headed back home sat across from me on the train that was to take me back home to our country. I slept a lot and then I just looked out the window and took in the beautiful countryside. They got off the train in Anspach and

I wished them well and thanked them for watching over me. The train pulled out again and headed towards Nuremberg. "Hauptbahnhof" the conductor announced as the train came to a complete stop. I spotted my Grandpa walking to see if he could spot me. I stuck my head out the window and waved at him. He came running, smiling with tears in his eyes saying "Helga, oh my Helga." He got on and hugged me. He couldn't believe his eyes, how I had grown. He took my suitcase off the shelf and we got off the train. He held the suitcase with one hand and my hand in the other, all the time exclaiming how happy he was to see me and that he couldn't wait for my Grandma to see me. We made our way out of the train station and headed towards a streetcar (Strassenbahn) that would take us to my grandparents' apartment in the South part of Nuremberg. I could not believe my eyes how the city had been rebuilt since we left about three years ago. It was unbelievable. I thought oh, Mom and Dad wouldn't believe this. We just have to move back home. They will be so surprised.

By now, we were at our destination. We got off the streetcar and walked a few feet to cross the street where on the other side we turned a corner and we could see the apartment building where my grandparents lived, Sperlingstrasse 9, up the street ahead. I could see my grandmother's head looking out of the window where she had been waiting and watching for us. She waved excitedly and then she disappeared. Since they lived in the apartment on the first floor it did not take her very long to come out in the street to meet us. She had a big smile on her face, and as I ran towards her, she closed me into her arms and she laughed and cried all at the same time. Then she was telling me how she missed me and how big I had gotten. (I was tall as she was then.) She kept on saying "I can't believe it." We made our way into the apartment where both of my grandparents tried to outdo each other by talking to me and hugging me until we were all three ready to sit down and take a deep relaxing rest. I could smell food. Grandma was a wonderful cook and she had made some of my favorite dishes for dinner, like a delicious homemade chicken noodle soup. She made her own noodles, was her soup ever delicious and so tasty. Then, there was homemade cheesecake, strawberries and cream. I ate so much that I thought my belly was going to explode. She loved watching me eat and so did my Grandpa. We sat around and talked a long time until it was time for bed.

They both had big plans for me for the weekend. They wanted all the neighbors to meet me, their friends and, naturally, all the other family members, my Great Grandmother who was still alive and well (She was my grandfather's mother.), then my uncle and aunt, cousins, great uncles and one great aunt (my Grandfather's sister). I had a wonderful time visiting with all of them, and we spent lots of good times together. Everyone wanted to invite us and fix a big dinner. We went for walks in the beautiful forests on weekends, rode boats on the lake, and we even visited the zoo. My Grandpa even took me along to his barber where he got his hair cut. He loved showing off his only granddaughter.

I started to bond with my first cousin Freddy who was six years old then. He was Uncle Robert and Aunt Frieda's only child. My Grandma used to have me take him up the street to a neighborhood park that also had a playground and play with him while she was busy cleaning and cooking. I didn't mind. I was always taught to listen and mind when I was told to do something. My Grandpa was still working. He was a salesman that sold artificial limbs for handicapped people. A lot of his business took him out of town, which he traveled those trips by train, and when he had some short trips for only half days, he took me along with him a couple of times. The one place we went to we carried our swimsuits. Grandpa told me that in the small town he had to go to there was an olympic-sized pool and whenever he got done taking care of his business, we would go swimming. I could not remember when I had been to such a nice large pool, and the water was so clear. I remember telling my Grandpa how I would love to stay all day. He laughed and we stayed pretty much all afternoon. We caught the 6 o'clock train home. My Grandma was worried. She said: "I didn't know what happened to you two, and I had to keep the food warm." Grandpa winked at me and said "Our little Helga had so much fun she forgot all about eating." That was so true. I loved going swimming.

Time seemed to fly by pretty fast, and I started missing my Mom and Dad. I was ready to go back home. My Grandfather was going to ride the train with me to the French border and then catch one back home to Nuremberg. Our goodbyes were sad and tearful, but I told my Grandparents that we would move back to Nuremberg real soon. It would probably be within a year, so that made it easier. My Grandpa cried when he got off the train and hugged me over and over. He told the conductor to please keep an eye on me. He, in turn, said he would. There were other people on the train that my Grandpa and I had been talking to and they were real nice people who traveled the same destination as I did, and they, too, told him they would watch out for me. I was pretty mature for my age and most people guessed me to be 15 or 16, when really I was just going on 13.

My Dad and Mom both picked me up in Sezanne at the train station and, again, it was an emotional welcome back since each of them were trying to get to me first, but my Dad did get my suitcase off the train which gave Mom a chance to get in her hugs and kisses. When we got back to the house, I got a really big surprise. Wow, there in the middle of the big kitchen floor sat a brand new creamy white with red and chrome trim bicycle. I couldn't believe my eyes. Now, it was my time for shedding tears, but they were tears of joy because I had wanted a new bike for a long time but never asked for one because I knew that both my parents had to really work hard, and they wanted to save up money so we could move back to Germany and get a nice apartment. So, I just kept my wishes to myself and kept on riding that old hand me down. But now, there it was right in front of me, a shiny brand new bike. I was getting restless and couldn't wait to take it outside to go for a ride, but since it had started to get dark outside, my Dad said that I should wait until the next day. Now that was really hard for me to do and I could hardly go to sleep. I was so excited in anticipation to break in that new bike. I hugged both my parents that night and thanked them over and over for that beautiful welcome home gift.

I woke up early the next morning in anticipation of riding my new bike. I asked Mom if she needed me to ride down the road to the farmhouse that sold eggs. That's where we bought all of ours. They were good fresh eggs and very reasonable. I had a basket that I hung on my handlebars and Mom put the money in it. Then, after my purchase, I headed back to the house with all the eggs in the basket. That was always done once a week on my old bike. Today, I would use my new bike and I was so excited. I wanted to run errands all day long just so I could ride. I had made lots of friends and most all of them rode bicycles, so we started to ride down the streets, then stand at a store corner and talk awhile before each of us had to go home.

Since my return from my vacation to Germany, there seemed to be some new boys in the group of teens, ages 14 – 17. There were three of them, all brothers and they were of Portuguese heritage. The older one of the three was very handsome and 17 years old. Gosh, I thought "is he handsome," that black wavy hair, sparkling brown eyes and whenever he smiled, he displayed two rows of perfect white teeth in a handsome suntanned face. I think I fell into my first "puppy love." His name was Bernard Pereira, but everyone called him "Bébé." Bébé seemed to have his eyes fixed on my face also. We both did a lot of glancing at each other. The fair came to town and we all went to have fun participating in rides, especially the bumper cars. My friend Colette and I rode together. We spotted Bébé and Michel. Naturally, we headed towards them in order to bump them, but they got to us first. We laughed lots and had fun.

After we were done with our rides we paired up and just walked through the fair, looking at all of the different booths and shows. All of a sudden a rain cloud came up. Bébé and I ran for cover and made it under a large maple tree. I leaned up against the tree and he had both arms stretched out standing straight in front of me as to protect me from the falling rain, but we didn't feel the wind or rain. We were looking deep into each other's eyes as his face seemed to get closer to mine. Then, it happened. He gave me my very first real kiss. I had never ever experienced the feelings I was having. It was a feeling I did not want to end. Finally, as the rain stopped, we came back down to reality. I suddenly worried that I would be late getting home and I told Bébé that I had to go. He held me by the hand and looked at me with such a serious look saying "I'll see you tomorrow." I answered my French "oui." I knew the love bug had bit me for the first time. Bébé and I saw each other every day and rode our bikes. I found out that he had five brothers and one sister. His grandparents still lived in Lisbon and sometimes some of the family would go and visit during summer vacations. All the boys in that family were very handsome. When I saw the sister for the first time her back was turned to me and she had beautiful long black hair.

Bébé didn't like it when I talked to other boys. He would question me why I spoke to this one or that one. That seemed to bother me for I liked talking to all my friends. Since Bébé and I became boyfriend-girlfriend, my 10- minute trips to the farm for egg shopping turned into one hour trips. We stopped near every tree and kissed. One day Mom was waiting on her eggs because she was in the middle of baking a cake and waiting on me to bring them back to the house. Whenever Bébé stood at the corner by the store talking to his friends and when he saw me pull out on my bike to head down the road, he would jump on his bike and follow me, so it took quite a while for me to deliver Mom's eggs in order for her to finish baking her cake. Don't think that I wasn't fussed at!

One day my Dad received a call from Germany and was offered a very good job. He and Mom talked it over and he made plans to go back to Nuremberg, take the job and find us an apartment, then Mom and I would follow.

We were all excited to go back home, back to our beloved Nuremberg, our families and friends that we had left behind. Yet, at the same time, I had very mixed feelings, leaving my friends that I had come to grow very fond of, France itself and, of course, my very first boyfriend whom I felt I really loved and now had to leave. A funny thing happened a couple of days before my Dad's departure. He and I went for a ride on our bikes. We rode side by side down a beautiful quiet road that was lined by big shade trees on each side. Dad was talking to me about being alone for a while with Mom and that I needed to help her with things, like grocery shopping, keeping the house clean, etc. I listened and promised to do as I was told. Suddenly, a Gendarme pulled us over with his lights flashing. We got off our bikes with a surprised look on our faces. We knew we were not speeding and most of all had not committed any sort of crime. He asked to see my Dad's papers. He did have an I.D. in his billfold. Then he asked how old I was. I told him 13; he said you look like 16! I shook my head. Then my Dad told him that I was his daughter and gave him my dates of birth and where we lived. He really did not believe us and asked us to park our bikes and get in his car. He needed to check things out. He really thought that my Dad wasn't my Dad, but just a young man trying to subdue a young girl. To me, that was just too funny and I had to laugh, but my Dad looked at me and I knew not to say anything back and to stop my laughing. So, to the police station we rode and when we got there he made several phone calls – one including my school teacher, Dad's work and the citizen's registrar. The worried Gendarme finally realized that the handsome young man was my Dad and the mature devel-oped13 year old was indeed his daughter, so he took us back tour bikes and we resumed our ride and had our talk. We couldn't wait to get home to tell mom about the incident. She laughed and shook her head saying "he must have been bored."

Dad started to pack up his things to get ready for his trip back to Germany. I felt so sad knowing that he was leaving and Mom and I would be on our own again, just like during and after the war. I cried and hugged my Dad. He gently stroked my hair, smiling and told me, "Helga, It won't be for long. I have to go and find an apartment for us to live in and start my new job. You and Mom will follow as soon as I take care of all that!" So, he left the next morning. Mom and I went to the train station with him and stayed until the train pulled out. Dad waved to us both and blew kisses, and we stayed, watched and waved until the train was out of sight. Mom and I went back to the house and we talked about how long it would be before we could get on a train to head back to our homeland. She tried to cheer me up and I her.

Time went by pretty fast. Mom kept her job at the factory and I was busy helping her with shopping for groceries and helping around the house with chores. She never did learn to speak French too well and had a hard time communicating or doing the shopping, so she wrote things down in German and I'd go get them. Most of the time she went along with me if we needed more than a few things for I couldn't carry it all. Mom had some German friends that we had met and still lived there, so they visited one another which gave her some distraction of being alone. Then, the people she worked with and had also befriended her kept in touch. I had my friends and, of course, had "Bébé." He started getting really sad each time he was around me and said that he didn't want me to leave and that he was afraid that I would have another boyfriend as soon as I got back to Germany. I told him that I would not and he could write me and perhaps he could come over for a visit. I really hated the thought at that time to leave him also. Gosh, he was so handsome. There were so many girls after him all the time, but during the time that he and I became close he seemed only interested in me.

He was just a little too jealous. Once I wore a wide elastic black belt around my waist with a floral flowing summer skirt and a tank top. My long hair was tied in a ponytail. As I rode down the street on my bike, all the boys were standing at their usual corner where they always met. As I passed, they whistled at me. Of course, Bébé was among them. He immediately jumped on his bike and caught up with me. We rode on down the road and he said to pull over. He looked pale and as though he was upset over something. He looked at me so serious and said: "Why are you wearing this belt to make your waist look so small?" I couldn't believe what I was hearing and first of all it made me laugh. That made him more angry. Then, I got angry and told him "It's just a belt that girls wear. What is your problem?" He then told me that I was driving the boys crazy and that one of his best friends had joined the French Foreign Legion because he was in love with me and could not stand to see me with Bébé. Then, I really bursted out laughing and told him that all the boys were crazy, so he jumped on his bike and left. We didn't speak or see each other for two days. I avoided riding by the corner where they met. The third day he followed me down to the farm where I was getting some eggs and butter for Mom and me. He looked at me so sad and asked if I was upset with him. I told him "no" that I was not upset, but I did not understand his actions. He then told me how much he loved me and he would never love anyone else the way he did me. He just couldn't stand it when other guys made complimentary remarks about me. Well, what could I say? He kissed me so passionately it sent trembles through my whole body. Somehow, I knew there would never be a future for us, but I knew in my heart that he was my first love. It never went beyond kissing. I was raised and I guess everyone else was in those days that sex was a sacred thing between a man and woman and not practiced as lightly and common as it has become in our present times. Back in those days and many years after, nice girls did not engage in sex until they were married.

We got a letter from my Dad almost every other day. In those days one didn't use telephones as much as today in order to communicate; that service was very expensive. Dad wrote that he liked his new job and made real good money, but he had to do some traveling as he worked as a representative for a company that sold this merchandise in lots of different parts of Germany.

He also wrote that he found an apartment close to the Nuremberg Castle and all we needed was to buy new furniture for it which he could do in about two to three more weeks, but he wanted Mom and I there so that we could help pick it out. Dad was staying with my grandparents since he went back. Those were good news. It meant that we were going back home, be a family again and enjoy all our relatives and old friends. But, it also meant leaving France and our new made friends, especially Bébé, but it was a good feeling, going home.

CHAPTER XI

LAST DATE AND GOODBYE

Bébé was really getting more and more depressed as our departure day for Germany was nearing. Mom had been packing lots of dishes, pots and pans, linens, towels and out of season clothing into boxes and mailed them ahead by transport. We just kept our clothes we needed and a few things that were of daily uses and necessities. Some things we would leave behind, perhaps some of our friends could use them after we were gone. They had commented that they would be glad to receive them.

The Sunday neared, that would be our last one in Sezanne. Bébé asked me if he could spend the afternoon with me since we were supposed to leave the next day around noon. Naturally, I asked mom if that was okay. She wanted to know what sort of plans we had. I told her riding bikes, going to a quiet place of nature and talk for a while. She thought for a moment, then agreed. She told me that she would see some friends and pack the rest of our things. So, Sunday after church and telling lots of my friends good-bye after the service, we went home and had some lunch. After I helped Mom to put things away and clean up, I got myself ready for my last date with Bébé. I really felt sad and sort of melancholic. The thought of not seeing him and riding our bikes together almost made me cry.

Bébé came by the house and waited outside on his turquoise-colored bike. It was a beautiful racing bike with lots of chrome and white trim. He wore a white polo shirt and jeans. His black hair was glistening in the sunlight. Mom came out with me and greeted him. "Hello Bébé!" He removed his sunglasses and smiled, exposing a beautiful row of perfect white teeth. Gosh, was he ever handsome! He replied "Hello Madame Gussmann, (how are you) Comment allez vous?" Mom's reply: "Merci, tres bien." He told her that he would take good care of me and have me back before dark. Mom looked at me saying in German, "Isn't that a bit long?" I said," Mom, it's our last day!" She said alright then but I don't think your Dad would want you go off too long. I said we are not doing nothing bad. We just want to talk and be together. Bébé kept looking from me to Mom. He had an idea what she was saying and again, he smiled his pretty smile, his tanned face, his hair, his masculine bone structure. He looked like a Roman or Greek Sun God. Of course, he was full-blooded Portuguese, so therefore the handsome Mediterranean features.

We rode our bikes down the streets that were lined by rows of beautiful shade trees on each side. We rode past farms and headed further out to a beautiful forest where a creek with sparkling clear water ran alongside of it. We got off our bikes and started to push them through part of the forest until we came to small lake that was midst a pasture of beautiful wild flowers. We sat down and talked. He told me about Portugal and his grandmother who still lived in Lisbon. He said he wanted me to go with him and meet her someday soon. He said that as soon as I turned 18 he wanted to marry me. "You can't date any German boys when you go back. Please wait for me!" I could not believe that he expected me to make such a commitment. I was still very young. After all, I still had several years of school ahead and I was not ready to make him this promise. I told him, "Bébé, wait and you come to visit me in Germany. There we'll see how it goes!" He put both arms around me and started to kiss me, first gently, then with such fire. We lay in the grass amidst beautiful wildflowers and kissed endlessly until finally I gazed at the sky and saw stars appearing. "Oh, Bébé, I have to go home. My Mom will be so angry with me. Look, it's almost dark!" Time had just completely gotten away from us both. It seemed that everything around us had disappeared. It was just he and I and those passionate kisses. To this day, I respect him as having been a complete gentleman and not having taken advantage of me, asking for any sexual favor. He was a very polite and religious young man. He was brought up by decent church-going Catholic parents, but he was passionate indeed. WE said goodbye at my house, both of us teary eyed. He promised to write and I promised the same. One long last kiss, "au revoir Cherie, au revoir Bébé." He worked the next day, so I knew that we would not see each other again.

Mom and I caught a bus around noon that was to take us to the train station. We had been very busy all morning getting ready and doing some last minute packing. I didn't get to see a lot of my friends, but some came to the corner when the bus left and hugged us goodbye. Finally, we were on the train that would take us both to Germany and all our family. I couldn't wait to see my Dad, Grandparents, aunts, and uncles. We slept on the train and we woke up early the next morning. It wasn't long until we pulled into Nuremberg.

CHAPTER XII

BACK HOME,
NEW BEGINNINGS

D ad was at the train station. I looked out of the window and saw him searching with his eyes until he saw me waving. I couldn't wait for the train to come to a stop. Dad got on board and after joyfully hugging mom and me, helped take our suitcases down from the upper shelf. There was lots to tell and talk about. We got a taxi and rode to my grandparents' house. Mom and I were amazed how Nuremberg had rebuilt from its ruins, our beautiful Nuremberg. Gee, it was good to be back home. My grandparents were looking out the window, watching for our arrival. As they lived on the first floor, it did not take them very long to come out and meet us when the taxi pulled up. Naturally, I was the first one to run up and hug them. They could not believe how I had grown since I had been there for a visit a year before. Now, we were all back home together. It was a great comforting feeling; family is a wonderful thing. My parents busied themselves the same day buying new furniture and preparing for the move to our apartment. It was all ready and fixed up within a couple of days, and I couldn't wait to have new furniture in my room. I had a day bed that could be used for a couch and a bed at night. We lived in the medieval part of town. I could see the castle from my bedroom window. What a beautiful sight! I strolled down the street where we lived. It was sort of a hillside. All the homes and businesses were on a hillside since the Castle itself had been built on the highest elevation of Nuremberg. Everything below was elevated then as it stretched out into a flat part and led right into the famous "Christkindles Market Central Market place where the beautiful "Frauenkirche" (Church) stood, the only surviving old building on the marketplace, the beautiful fountain (Schoner Brunnen) that rises to 60 feet in the form of a filigreed Gothic church tower. It was erected in the second half of the 14th century. The Frauenkirche became world famous and thousands of tourists visit each day to watch at noon in front of the church for the figure clock to strike. After the hours are tolled, the trumpeters lift their instruments, then the half round figures under the dial begin to move, and finally the doors open to reveal the red clad princes who parade three times around the emperor. It is truly an amazing, unique and pleasant performance to watch. The Market Place itself is a fruit, vegetable and flower market, open pretty much all year. However, it becomes very colorful during the Christmas Season, starting December 1st through Christmas Eve when toys Zwetschgermannlein, golden angels, Christmas ornaments, breads, Lebkuchen and all conceivable sorts of Nuremberg products are sold in wooden stalls of the Christkindles market. We lived in walking distance of five minutes to the Central Market and the same up to the castle from our apartment. I enrolled in the Paniersplatz School which was located on the opposite side of the castle to finish out the 7th grade school year.

I need to mention that I had been getting several letters from Bébé with a 3 x 6 picture of himself wearing a white V-neck sweater with blue and red trim. Of course, I had been writing to him as well and had also sent him a picture of myself. He said that he missed me terribly and rode by the lonely, empty house we used to live in.

I had quite an experience starting back to school again in the German language after all the years having been educated in French which I spoke fluently and accent free when I left France. My last year in school there I proudly made the Honor Roll with having a beautiful proclamation made by the school's principal. She gave out the year's end report cards in our classroom and asked me to stand. I didn't know what she was going to say to me and waited anxiously as she went over my report card. Then, she looked at all of the pupils in the classroom and started her speech. It went something like this: "I want you all to look at this girl and use her for a role model. She came to this country not speaking a word of French, but she worked really hard. Now, she speaks as well as any French girl or boy and made the Honor Roll with only a few others from this class room." Then she said, "Helga, we are all so very proud of you and we shall miss you when you leave us, but we wish you the best and a bright future. I know you will make something special out of your life." I thanked her and could feel all the eyes staring at me. Some of my friends came up and hugged me. The principal and my teacher also gave me a hug. So now, meeting a whole classroom full of German girls and teacher, truly felt like an odd ball and it was a bit scary. I was nervous the first day, but everyone made me feel welcomed and I had a wonderful little teacher. She was very short, 4'10" and had never ever married. She was in her late 40's, smiled and was very pleasant and patient with her students. She was Fraulein Mockel. Upon my first entering the new class room, I was the center of attraction for days to come. I was asked to speak and sing French. All sorts of questions were asked daily and I answered the best I could.

I didn't have any problems falling into the academics. I had been speaking and reading lots of German books in my absence from Germany, so I never made any bad grades. My favorite subjects had always been history, geography, science, religion and language. Math was one of my less favorites. I never failed the subject but never wound up with A's, usually C's. But I can add, subtract, multiple. I disliked fractions and algebra.

One day I brought a picture of Bébé to school and showed it to my classmates. Their reactions were "Oh, my gosh, what a handsome guy he is. You are a very lucky girl." I said, "Oh well, we are just good friends." To my surprise, on the very next day three of my friends brought pictures of themselves and asked me to send them to Bébé. I couldn't believe what I was hearing and seeing. I had to laugh, but I told them that I would send him the pictures in order for them to leave me alone about Bébé. I thought it would be funny to send him the pictures and let him know how crazy the girls in my class were about his good looks, so I did. When he answered my letter, he sent the pictures back and asked if I wanted to be rid of him. He didn't like it at all, and he took it in another way, whereas, I had meant it to be funny and complimentary. Oh well, somehow we didn't see eye to eye on many things and we lived a long way apart, so the letters between us became fewer and fewer. Meanwhile, he entered the military and went through some tough basic training. He stayed very busy and I was very busy studying at school and making new friends, but I didn't date any boys until I turned 15.

I met a girl at school who became my best friend for life, Renate. She was an only child, just as I was then. She had a brother who died at age 15 during a bomb attack in the war. Her father was also killed fighting during World War II, so she lived alone with her Mom, Mrs. Erhardt. She was the sweetest little mother, always a smile for anyone. She told me that I was her other daughter and gave me a hug. Renate and I became as close as sisters. We spent weekends at each other's house, walked to and from school together. We didn't live far apart from one another. We would go to movies and school dances. We went to camp for a week from school. Of course, our bunks were in the same dorm; we became inseparable. Whenever we went to movies with a couple of boys, it was with two friends, just so we could be together. We both took the same classes – typing, shorthand, and bookkeeping. Then, in the ninth grade we took some English classes. We went to our first job and trained at the same time while still being in high school. School and work, my first job was to learn how to accurately file. I did this for a whole month, then, came typing some business letters that I had taken down in shorthand. Bookkeeping followed next. Renate went to work for an insurance company. It turned out that she would stay there until she retired as office manager over 51 employees. She was very smart. I worked for a large manufacturing company that made shaving brushes. They shipped them all over the world. I stayed there one year. Later, I worked for a cloth manufacturer that mostly sold their merchandise to local and out of town taylors. All in all, it was a good learning experience for me.

I really wanted to do to work for Air France Air lines. Back then, it was really difficult wanting to become an airline stewardess. Now they are called flight attendants. First of all, you had to have a certain height and weight, attractive looks and most of all, lots of training that required one- year ground service and the qualification to speak five languages – English, French, Italian, Spanish and German – because those were the countries most frequently traveled and in order to serve all passengers with the utmost service those things were required. During the first year of ground service, it was all about first aid, courtesy, foreign languages, etc. It gave each girl that polished look and elegant poise. My parents were not that enthused about my decision. My Dad suggested I become a translator of languages. I seemed to have an excellent talent of learning foreign languages and my pronunciation was very good. Or, he said, how about working in a dental lab. I said "dental lab, a make false teeth? No way Daddy." Mom thought that I should keep working In an office as a secretary. They both tried to talk me out of going into the aviation because they were afraid that I could get killed in a plane crash. Mom was still working at the Triumph Typewriter Company and Dad was a sales representative for artificial limbs.

Dad noticed an ad in the paper. Someone was looking for a couple to manage a family restaurant. It was located in Eibach, outside of Nuremberg. The three of us went to Eibach and checked it out. It was in a nice location across from a beautiful pine forest. After Mom and Dad checked everything out they seemed to like it and decided to give it a try. They signed a two-year lease and made arrangements to take it over. The restaurant had an apartment above that was to become our new home. So, we gave up the apartment in town. Mom and Dad quit their job and we went into the restaurant business. My Mom always loved to cook and bake, so therefore it was a pleasant change for her. She got paid for what she loved doing. Business kept picking up and we did well. Soon, we had regular customers. They all seemed to enjoy Mom's cooking. I helped to wait on tables when I was there on weekends and out of school. After a couple of months, Mom and Dad had to hire extra help for weekends. It was hard work and they put in lots of long hours, but the income was really prosperous. We had a piano in the restaurant and Mom decided that I should take lessons. She knew a lady who lived a couple streets away who taught piano and she agreed to come to our restaurant once a week in early morning before opening and give me lessons. Well that lasted a long three months. The teacher and I didn't see eye to eye. She wanted me to learn all the notes and read music. I wanted to play by ear, so I just stopped taking lessons altogether. Today, I wish I hadn't.

Next to our restaurant lived a real nice middle-aged couple. They had a nephew who had defected from East Germany and came to live with them. He was 17 years old and trained to be a boxer. His name was Werner, but everybody called him Bobby. Pretty soon, Bobby became friends with Renate and I. We three just started hanging out together. We went to movies, Mardi gras dances, hiking. Renate and I even joined Bobby on his runs while he was training. We also went along to boxing events to watch him box. What we didn't like was the blood and there were lots of bloody noses. Bobby was like our brother, and his aunt and uncle were real sweet people and good neighbors. Quite often they sent vegetables from their garden or Bobby would reach across the fence when he saw me outside behind the restaurant smiling and handing me a bouquet of flowers that he had just picked from his aunt's flower garden. He always made me laugh. Renate came out lots on weekends. She and I used to join him on his runs through the forest. He was training to get in shape. Naturally, our energy did not last as long as his, so we just sat down and waited for him. This always resulted in a big tease from him, but we just laughed it off. Renate and I were always invited whenever he had a real boxing match, but we just didn't like the roughness and the blood, especially when it came from Bobby's nose. He would laugh at both of us and say, "You two had better get used to that. You'll be seeing lots more of that whenever you watch any boxing match. We just looked at each other and shook our heads, saying "We may not get to go every time." Bobby just smiled and gave us a hug.

Another young man by the name of Manfred, who also lived in Eibach, became friends with the three of us while we were finishing one of our runs in the forest. He looked sort of like a "nerd." He was skinny, tall and had slicked-back dark hair. He wore black horn-rimmed eye glasses, but real nice and friendly, surely a total opposite of Bobby. He told us that he worked in an office as a sales representative but that on weekends he was the leader of a five-piece band and where he played a clarinet, horn, etc. He said that they play at a coffee house in downtown Nuremberg every Sunday afternoon and we should try and come down some Sunday. So, we took him up on his invitation and went to Nuremberg the following Sunday afternoon. We sat down and ordered coffee and some delicious pastries that were a specialty there. We listened to the music and we really enjoyed the type of music that they were playing. It was good listening and dancing music. When the band took a break, Manfred came over and sat with us. He thanked us for coming, then in a conversation pertaining to music and singing, Renate and Bobby volunteered the information to Manfred that I was a good singer and that I could even sing French and English. "On no," I thought, "here we go." After all three of them bombarded me with their pleadings, I agreed to do my two songs. I sang "C'est si Bon" in French, and then the only English song I knew all of the words to was "You are my Sunshine, My Only Sunshine," believe it or not, but I was eagerly applauded. (Heaven only knows why.) So, from time to time I would sing with the group whenever we went to listen to them. We had fun between that and going to movies and some of Bobby's boxing matches. The rest of the time was spent working very hard, helping out in the restaurant and going to school and working. Working while still going to school helped to finish my high school education a lot quicker because you learned the business while you studied.

At the same time, I heard that an elderly professor who lived two blocks away from our restaurant gave private English lessons out of his home. He was in his early 80s and lived by himself with a housekeeper that came in each day to cookk and do his household chores. He told me that he used to teach at the University of Heidelberg in his younger days. When I asked him if he would teach me a couple of hours a week, he agreed, after getting my parents' permission. I started my English lessons with great anticipation. He was such a sweet old man and he even taught mean old English song: "Oh, it's a long way to Tipperary." He and I would sing it each time after I finished my English lession.

Renate and I were still taking English lessons at school as well plus advanced courses in typing, shorthand and bookkeeping. We had some good laughs, learning English with British pronunciation. It sounded so different from the way the Americans talked. I had met several American families that were stationed in Nuremberg due to military occupancy. The higher rank military personnel and their families lived in some of the most beautiful villas, some that previously belonged to upper class Nazis that now were spending the biggest or even remaining time of their lives in prison. I have always been so fascinated by the American people, their way of life, their language, the beautiful colorful clothes they wore, the large cars that they drove, and, most of all, I loved their food. The German economy was on the rise and by now there were plenty of jobs, new homes and food was now also plentiful. The German spirit seemed to be blossoming again and people seemed to enjoy life, looking forward to a brighter future. The hard times we went through were gone, but not forgotten. They taught me and most everyone else that experienced those hard and meager years to appreciate the daily needs for life, not to be wasteful, but be thankful for everything that God gives you. I have eaten leftover foods all of my life and still do today, and I will until my life is over. We should never take anything for granted. It truly is a blessing to have a roof over your head, a warm bed to sleep in and enough food to keep your body satisfied. The very thought of any human being having to do without these necessities is truly heartbreaking, especially when it comes to the elderly, the children and the sick.

My English vocabulary was growing rapidly. I was proud of every word that I learned and I tried to talk to someone in English whenever I had a chance. I know that I had (and still have) quite a bit of accent, but that didn't stop me from learning more and more. I listened to American radio stations. I listened to the songs and tried to sing them.

Our restaurant business seemed to be taking its toll on Mom and Dad's personal and family lives. We could not do anything together anymore. Either Dad would take a night off and go to see a boxing match with his brother Robert or both my grandpa included. Mom would take time off to visit her sisters, aunts or cousins in Nuremberg. Business was very good and prosperous but one of them always had to be there and they missed having a personal life, so after two years Mom and Dad decided to sell out and move back to Nuremberg. It took a few months to find a new place to live and Mom and Dad getting new jobs, but it all fell into place and we moved to Adam Klein Strasse, 75 Nuremberg. It was not very far from the Justiz Gebaude (Palace of Justice) where all of the trials of Nuremberg occurred after World War II and all the war criminals brought to justice for the horrendous war crimes they had committed. Mom and Dad seemed to enjoy working for someone else again and having their evenings and weekends to themselves. I was still in school and worked several days a week, but it was fun now not having to catch the train or bus to come into Nuremberg. Bobby hated to see us move away but could come and visit, which he did now and then, but we didn't see each other as much as we used to. We all had busy lives.

CHAPTER XIII

DATE WITH AN AMERICAN SOLDIER

I finished my training in shorthand, typing and book-keeping. I was also accomplished in general office work. Summer came and I headed for the pool as often as I could with the weather being permissible. Sometimes I would meet with friends and other times when no one else could join me I would go by myself. I loved the sun, liked getting a tan and enjoyed swimming. On one such day when I went alone, I sat on my beach towel looking at some American comic books that a friend of mine who was an American lady named Helen had given me in order that I could practice my newly learned language. Anyway, after some time, I noticed three American GIs spreading their beach towels on the ground not far from where I sat, listening. I could hear them talking, but I did not understand too much of what they were saying, something like that beauty in that black bathing suit. I did have on a one-piece black bathing suit, but I disregarded the comment and kept looking at one of the books. It was not very long until one of them came over and introduced himself as "Jim." He was tall and quite nice looking with light brown hair, brown eyes and he sported a muscular tanned body. He smiled and then asked if he could borrow one of my comic books, so I handed him a couple and smiled back at him. After he went back to the other two GIs and sat down on his towel, I noticed he flipped the pages but all the while he kept looking my way, so I just got up and headed towards the olympic-size pool and got in the water for a swim. I heard some whistles as I walked towards the pool, but I did not look around. It was not long until I had some company. Yes, all three got into the pool as well. Two of them swam in the other direction while the Jim guy swam over towards me grinning from ear to ear. Then he started saying a lot of (heaven only knows what). I finally asked him in my limited English if he could speak German or French. He said, "One moment" and he took off to fetch one of his friends. He introduced me to him. He was a dark-haired, olive-skinned guy and said, "bonjour Mademoiselle, comment allez vous?" I replied, "bonjour, je suis tres bien." So, here started our three-way conversation. Jim told him in English to ask me (which was in French) if I would like to have dinner with him in a German Restaurant. I thought about it a moment and told his friend to tell Jim that I would go whenever he was free from his military duties one evening. He said he could go the next evening, so after giving him a familiar place as to where we could meet, we said good bye and we all started for home as it was getting to be late afternoon.

I told my parents that I was meeting some new friends to go out and have dinner with. I told them that they were Americans and that I would be right back home after we ate. They trusted me and they knew that I loved being around Americans, but they also knew that I knew my rules and limits and always had to be home at a certain time. So, I got dressed up the next evening and caught a street car that took me to the Hauptbahnhof (train station) which was right in the center of the city. There was a large stone column that had a clock on all four sides. I was to meet them at 7 o'clock. Seven it was, and I saw Jim and his French speaking friend, Charles. Well, they both smiled and shook hands. They also complimented my hair and dress and told me how pretty I was. I thanked them and pointed down the street where all sorts of shops and nice restaurants were located. I told them about some that served some really good German food, and so we headed down the street with not one but two GIs. Hmm, I wondered. People must think I really like these guys. We arrived at the restaurant and were seated. Jim sat next to me, Charles across from both of us. We looked at the menu. Charles asked me what I was going to choose for my meal, so I told him. Then he told Jim. He, in turn, told him that he wanted to order the same things. I couldn't help smiling and thinking of it as being very funny.

We had a nice evening speaking in our foreign languages. After a while, I told my two new friends that it was time for me to go back home. So, after they paid for our meal, they walked me back to where I had to catch a streetcar that stopped close by where I lived. They asked could they accompany me, but I politely told them no, that I would be okay. I certainly did not want my neighbors looking out of their windows and see me walking up with a GI on each side of me. That would have started some neighborhood gossip. Charles and Jim went out with me for walks and dinner. After that, Jim decided the two of us would get along just fine without him. He told me that he played some football in the military against other teams. It was out by the stadium where he was stationed at the Merrell Barracks. It had been a former German base for soldiers, mostly Hitler's SS troops. Now, it was occupied as a military base by the Americans. I understood him to say that I should come out there Tuesday afternoon and watch the game. I agreed that I would be there Tuesday. I got myself ready, caught a streetcar and headed towards soldiers' field where the game was supposed to take place. He had even told me the number jersey he would be wearing, so I was getting excited. I had never ever seen an American football game. I got off the streetcar and started walking towards the stadium and to my surprise did not hear a noise nor was there a single soul in the stadium. I stopped in my tracks. Then it hit me. Why the nerve of this guy. He just plain lied to me and stood me up. I whirled around and headed back to catch the next streetcar that was to take me back home. I didn't hear anything from Jim or anyone else that day or the next. On Friday, I received a phone call from Charles. After exchanging hellos and how do you do, he asked me for Jim, in French, why I did not come to yesterday's game. I said "Yesterday, you mean Thursday?" He said "yes." I told him "Oh, I thought he said Tuesday. I went out there and he was not there." Charles started laughing and then he said no, it was Thursday. So, it was a misunderstanding, mostly mine. Tuesday and Thursday sound a lot alike. There were other misunderstandings, mostly because of the language barrier.

Jim was a very likeable and well-mannered guy. So, one day I introduced him to my parents and they, too, took a liking to him. He told us that he was born and raised in Tennessee and that he had only one sister named Mary. She was married to a man named Ken who then served in the U.S. Air Force, making it a career. They had a small little girl named Debbie. He told me that his parents lived on a farm and raised tobacco. My parents, grandparents, uncles and aunts and friends would drive to the country on weekends. My Dad owned a motor scooter and also a car, a DKW, so we would all visit some of our relatives or go for long walks in the woods. Then, after stopping at a restaurant for an early evening meal we would head back home. We started to invite Jim to come along whenever he was off that week-end, and he seemed glad to come along. He told me that he had written to his parents and told them about me. He said, "They got the pictures I sent them and they think you are a very beautiful girl."

CHAPTER XIV

JACK AND JILL
WENT UP THE HILL

We were on a weekend outing with my parents while they visited with family and friends. Jim and I would go for walks in the beautiful countryside. We carried a blanket that we could spread out under a tree and sit there and talk. This particular day I did not bring a blanket but Dad had a sleeping bag in the trunk. We decided to bring it along and then started on our walk. After climbing up a steep hill we found a shady place under a tree. The view was splendid and very picturesque. Jim unzipped the sleeping bag, spreading it on the ground. There we talked and laughed and, yes, kissed. After letting out a laugh, Jim said, "I just thought of something funny. Let's see if we both fit inside the sleeping bag and zip it up. I said, "Oh no, I am claustrophobic. I can't stand being squeezed into real tight spaces." He laughed and said it would not hurt anything. We would come right back out of it. I said okay but make it fast. He zipped the darn thing up all of the way to our necks with only our heads exposed. I started wiggling saying "Get me out of here." Well, the bag started to move and before we could stop it, it was rolling down the hill with each of us tumbling over one another, finally coming to a stop right next to the road. It felt like two wieners between a bun. Neither of us were able to move. Our legs and arms seemed to be stuck in there. Of all things to happen, a car was nearing. They slowed down and curiously looked down at us. What sight we must have been. The guys in the car were grinning and whistling, then went on. I was so embarrassed I was almost crying, and I thought I was going to die if I did not get out of this contraption that I was in. Jim, finally realizing that he had a very panicked and hysterical girl to deal with, tore the zipper open and out we came. I was furious and so upset with Jim. I would not talk to him the rest of the day. He told everyone back at our relatives' house what had happened. Everybody was laughing so hard. My Dad did come over and put his arm around me and told the rest of the clan to leave me alone. Jim apologized but I just looked at him and nodded. I didn't even kiss him when he left to go home. I turned my head and closed the door. He called the next day and invited me to go to a movie on base. I agreed and went to meet him at Merrell Barracks the next evening. Afterwards, we had dinner at the snack bar and then headed to the bowling alley located on base as well. We both seemed to have fun. I loved bowling. Jim seemed very good at it. He bowled in a league on base. I threw quite a few gutter balls, being just my first time to bowl. We started to socialize with other military couples that seemed to be helping me to carry on more and more to converse using the English language.

It was now late summer and Jim confessed to me that he loved me and wanted to marry me. He told me that he had to leave the following year in April to go back to the states and he wanted me to come home with him. His three-year military time would come to an end. I have to be honest; I was a little bit disappointed to hear that he was getting out of the military. I sort of liked military life.

I knew that we would get to travel and see different countries, but Jim wanted out and "be free." He wanted to hunt and fish whenever he wanted, not when the military told him he could. I knew that I would finish with my school that spring also, so it would work out okay. After all, that is what I had wished for all of my life, going to America. Yes, yes. I was ready to leave and start a new life. I knew I was very young and should have gone on to the university and study a few years in order to have a good career, but I really wanted to move on. Mom and I did not see eye to eye on many things. It seemed like everything I did or tried to do was always wrong. I could never please her. Dad always took up for me but then the two of them would get into it. She got really angry with me a couple of times and told me to get out, so I moved in with my aunt for a few weeks until she got over her mad spell and told me to come back home. All of this with Mom and me not getting along helped me to decide to start paperwork for me and Jim to get married. I really felt a lot for him and felt that we would have a good marriage and that we both could have some beautiful children. Mom was all for me getting married, but since I was not 18 yet she had to sign the papers and give permission. The same thing had to be done by my Dad. He would not sign. He said that I was too young, not quite 17. He was right, of course, but I thought that I was old and smart enough to know what I wanted and that everything would work out alright.

There were a few things that bothered me. Jim had told me that when he went back to the states on a furlough his parents gave a big party and invited lots of people – friends and family. There was a young girl that he met and liked very much. So much that he bought her an engagement ring and gave to her before going back to Germany. He really fell hard for her and I could tell when he talked about her that he still seemed to care some. He even showed me her picture, and she, too, was pretty, but soon after Jim returning to Germany she met someone else that she loved more than Jim so she broke off the engagement and got married to the other man. This hit Jim very hard, so I think that he kind of met me on the rebound. Another time, Jim got cold feet about getting married, but he did not come out and tell me. Instead, he made up some horrible story and told me that they had found a spot on his lung that looked like it was going to grow and there was probably nothing they could do, so he did not have much time. I actually became so worried and upset that I called up his Master Sergeant crying. I asked him how bad was he really off and wasn't there anything that could be done for him. At that point I was not concerned about marrying him but about saving his life. To my amazement, the nice Sergeant said "There is not a single thing wrong with Savage" and "did he honestly tell you this?" I told him that he did and that I had been crying my heart out for him thinking that he was going to die. Why, that son of a gun. Wait until I talk to him. Well, I got a visit from Jim that night. He was very apologetic and told me that he had been getting letters from home telling him not to marry some foreign girl and bring her back to the states, especially her being of the Catholic faith. He went to a church in the country called Zion Chapel. I guess it was of the protestant faith. That experience put a different feeling in my heart. I started to become very doubtful about things. Mom did not make things any easier for me. I never told her and Dad about the other girl in his life nor did I tell them about the lie that was told to me.

After lots of arguing from my Mom with my Dad, he finally signed the papers, and we started the proceedings to be married. It was not easy and we had stacks and stacks of papers to fill out. My background was thoroughly checked out to make sure that no one in my family was a Nazi or a communist. Then, I had to travel to Munich by train to be checked through the American Consul. A complete medical exam was performed. I remember until this day when my blood was drawn for the first time I was so scared that I almost passed out. An American soldier and his wife who happened to be in the same exam room said "Honey, look at that poor girl's face. Why it is as white as my shirt."

In November 1956, our paper work was finally completed. I was issued a certificate and passport to marry and enter the USA. I was so excited. I thought, I finally get to go to America. I was so happy I cried. Mom and I started to shop for my wedding dress. We went to a real nice bridal shop, and after trying on several different styles I went with a long sleeve, lace upper top consisting of a high neck. The bottom was made of a taffeta full shirt with an overlay of tulle. My headpiece was a princess crown from which cascades a long veil. It was a beautiful dress.

CHAPTER XV

WEDDING BELLS

We had to get married at the courthouse on November 24th and then had the church wedding on Saturday, the 26th. Previous to our wedding we had to meet with the Priest. He asked Jim would he be interested in becoming a Catholic. Jim said he had not made up his mind. Then the Priest asked him would he object to our children being baptized and becoming Catholic just as their mother, and he replied no, he would not object to our children being baptized and brought up in the Catholic faith. I was glad to hear that. My faith and religion mean a whole lot to me.

Our wedding day was nearing. I picked two flower girls, a ring boy and my matron of honor who was one of my cousins. Jim picked a friend from his company, Jack Albright, to be his best man. As I mentioned before, we were legally married on November 24th by law at the courthouse. Then, on the 26th was to be our church wedding. There were probably around 100 people attending. I rode to the church from my house with my parents in a black chauffeured Mercedes Benz. Jim was waiting at the church. The Catholic Church was just three blocks up the street from where I lived. The chauffer got out and opened our doors. As I got out I could hear the church bells ringing loud. It could be heard all over the neighborhood. People were lined in the streets and on each side of the steps going up to church to get a good look at the bride and the proud Mom and Dad. Both walked in with me. I saw my grandparents rising up from their seat and smiling at me, yet at the same time teary eyed. I heard exclamations: "Oh, she is so beautiful" or "What a beautiful bride." I was trembling and shaking I was so nervous. I knew that I was taking a big step in my life and knew I would be leaving all of this behind. My family, friends, and, of course, my country, to go to a place I had never been and meet new people I did not know. I sort of became overwhelmed and it took all of my effort to hold back the tears that started to come from my eyes. Then, I realized, by law I was already married to the man that I was about to give my vows to again before God and all who were present. So, I kept on walking and sort of smiling at everyone that caught my glance.

The Priest performed the lengthy ceremony that is so customary in a Catholic wedding. After the ceremony people stood in line to congratulate us as we headed for the exit, especially from Jim's company. So many GIs and most of them in uniform. We had our reception given by my parents at a restaurant near our neighborhood. It was a full, sit-down meal with a wedding cake and coffee to follow. Afterwards, a band played for a dance that lasted into the night. Everyone seemed to have a real good time. A neighbor of ours who was also a guest at the wedding came up to me and said "You sure are a beautiful bride, and I always heard that it is bad luck if rain falls on a bride's veil." Rain it did the day we were married. I just sort of smiled and replied "Well, maybe that will not apply to me Mrs. Wurm." She said "You know that I always wished you to become my daughter in law." Her son Helmut and I had just been good friends. There was no any romantic intention, at least not on my part.

For some strange reason, several of the guys from Jim's company decided they wanted a piece of my wedding dress for a souvenir, so they started to cut a small piece off the bottom of my dress, which was the overlay tulle of my skirt, and stuck it in their billfold. I thought, some strange custom, maybe that is what they do in the states. I never heard of that being done ever again anywhere. Oh well, I hope it brought all of them good luck.

Jim had six more months left of his time to be in Germany and also to be in the Army until his time was completed. Having six months left to be around my parents, we decided to stay with them until our departure for the states. I started to receive a monthly soldier's spouse check from the U.S. Government, and I could shop in all of the military-operated facilities, such as the commissary, BX, patronize all on base entertainment, bowling alley, snack bar, club, and I could use the medical facility as well. I sort of felt superior getting to attend all of those things that I used to dream about as a young girl and now I even had become a Mrs.

Pretty soon, I was finally getting to go to my so much wished for destination U.S.A. As I had mentioned earlier, I had become friends with several Americans. Also, Jim had introduced me to three of the wives from friends in his company. They all had been to our wedding. Mary Lou, Judy and Dottie taught me several of the American ways, especially shopping. Oh yes, I will never forget the very first time I got to go to the commissary to shop for groceries. I now had a pass where I could go and do all of that. I felt so special. The girls came with me and showed me where things were that I needed. We had taken a bus that took us to the base, but after I got done with m shopping and had all of those bags of groceries, we had to call a cab to take us home. It seems funny today. Yes, they were all my groceries. I guess I sort of went crazy going for the very first time. I did not even remember what all I bought or if I knew what I bought, but I had a blast. I enjoyed eating all of those delicious American foods.

Christmas neared. It was our first one as a married couple. We started receiving Christmas cards from the states. They were all from his family which was quite large when it came to aunts, uncles and cousins. His brother in law, Ken, who was in the U. S. Air Force and stationed in France at the time came for a visit. Ken was a very nice and outgoing person and told me that he welcomed me into the family. He had been married to Jim's sister Mary for around three years. As I had mentioned earlier, they had a two-year old girl named Debbie and expecting another one soon. Mom and Dad also liked Ken and enjoyed his company. He stayed only a few days and then had to leave. By that time, we had become good friends and seemed to get along well. Speaking of friends, I noticed that some of my friends had started to alienate themselves from me. They knew that by having married an American soldier I would be leaving soon and that they would probably never see me again. My best friend, Renate, seemed to have grown sort of sad each time we saw each other, which was very seldom now that I had a husband that came home every night, but she was still my friend and we talked about how we would write to one another and eventually see each other again. Naturally, I felt sort of sad knowing that I would not get to see her and talk to her probably for a very long time.

The first of January arrived and it was a very cold month. One day during that month the temperature dropped to 36 degrees below zero.

My Dad was approached by a company that was a distributor for beers and soft drinks. They wanted him and Mom to take over a new location in Nuremberg to deliver to restaurants, stores and other places where beers and drinks were sold. It had a newly built house including an office and two trucks for the delivers. After he and Mom talked it over they decided to take it. Mom was to take care of the office work and Dad help with deliveries. They hired a couple of drivers and their new business was on its way. We all helped with the moving. I had moved so much during my childhood that this seemed the normal thing to do. During all of this moving going on, Mom did not feel too good and was nauseated almost every day. After lots of pleading from my Dad and me, she went to see her family doctor. He examined her and ran some tests. It turned out that Mom was about two months pregnant, after all these years, so Mom must have gotten pregnant around the time when I was married. I could hardly believe all of this was happening and we were having to leave in the month of April to come to the states. That meant that I would not be here in August when my little brother or sister was being born. This really saddened me as for all my life I had wished for a younger brother or sister and now I would not even be here when the baby came.

We really liked living in the new house. It had a large kitchen, dining room, two bedrooms, bathroom and an office. The business was doing great. It paid well and Mom and Dad seemed to like running it. My grandparents did not live to too far away from our new home and they came by to visit us quite often. As the time neared for my departure to the states, I started to have mixed emotions. A part of me was excited and could not wait to get to my new home. On the other hand, I felt very sad having to leave my parents, grandparents, friends, other family members, and I was very worried having to leave my Mom to deliver another baby after a seventeen-year gap since she had me. But, I had made my choice and now I had to deal with all of my mixed emotions. : Looking back now, I realize that I was so young to take on all that was coming at me even though I had always been very mature for my age.

The Army came and packed all of our possessions – dishes, silverware, china and other items – most all were wedding gifts. Also, there were lots of items from my Hope Chest. My Mother had started one for me several years earlier. It contained linens, towels and tablecloths. The day for our departure was approaching. I tried to act happy and cheerful around all of my family, especially Mom and Dad. Inside, I was very nervous, meeting my new in laws, adjusting to new ways and customs. Jim kept telling me that everything would be fine and I would like it where he came from and that his family was looking forward to meeting their daughter-in-law. I knew in my heart that I loved Jim and he was now my husband. I felt that he would be there for me, protecting me and being supportive no matter what would happen, yet I felt fearful for all the unknown and where I would not know anyone besides Jim and my new brother-in-law Ken who by now was already back in the states and stationed at the Smyrna Air Force Base which was also located in Tennessee and about a 30 to 40 minute drive from Greenbrier where Jim's parents lived on a farm. By government orders the Smyrna Air Force Base was closed years later and served as a private air strip.

We started to get dinner invitations from friends and families, lots of delicious foods, many hugs and some tears were also shed. Promises were made of writing letters and then sometimes in our future we would see each other again.

Our last night had arrived. We had to get up early the next morning. Our suitcases were packed and loaded into the trunk of my Dad's car. My grandparents, aunts and uncles came by also. My grandparents promised to come to the train station the next morning to tell us goodbye. I hugged them teary eyed and told them that would make me very happy. After they left to go home and Jim went on to bed, I sat up with both of my parents and we talked for a long time. I was given lots of helpful advice, but I was also told that if things did not work out for me that I should let them know and they would do their best to get me back home. They told me that they loved me and that they were also very proud of me and the young woman I had become. I went to bed but I lay there for a long time before falling in to a restless sleep! It seemed like no time until a shrill alarm from the bedside alarm clock went off and the time had come to get ready for my long anticipated trip.

CHAPTER XVI

VOYAGE TO MY
DESTINATION

We got dressed and ate a small breakfast of German rolls, boiled eggs, butter, jelly and coffee. I could barely eat a half of a roll and I drank my coffee, then we walked out the door.

I took one last look before getting into Dad's car. Jim sat up front and Mom and I sat in the backseat. My grandparents were coming by streetcar to meet us at the Nuremberg train station. My heart was beating so fast I could feel it in my chest and clear up in my throat. Then, I started shaking all over. What on earth was the matter with me? I pulled myself together, took a deep breath and started smiling as big as I could. We all started to go up to the rail station from where our train was to leave for Bremerhaven. Jim and my Dad carried our suitcases and loaded them onto the waiting train. They emerged and we all stood there hugging, crying and saying goodbyes. The conductor's loud voice said "Alles Einsteigen (everyone aboard)." One last squeeze and hug and we got on the train. We opened the window and talked to everyone while waiting for the train's wheels to set in motion. My sweet grandpa reached up for my hand and holding on to it he started walking along with the train as it was set in motion and picking up speed. Tears were rolling down his face as he kept saying: "I love you little Helga, take care." I finally had to move my hand. I was afraid he would start walking too fast and fall, but we waved to each other until all were out of sight.

I looked around at our compartment. It was just for the two of us with a table by the window and one side were two bunk beds. Jim was trying to make me laugh by saying funny things about us sleeping together on the upper bunk. "Oh no, no way. I am sleeping on the bottom and you sleep on the top" was my reply. We sat by the window looking out at the picturesque countryside for a long time until we were served our evening dinner. We then got ready and climbed in our bunks, being very tired. The humming sound soon made us fall asleep.

The train pulled into Bremerhaven early the next morning. A waiting bus took us to a U.S. Army Military Base. We had to have all of our paperwork, belongings, and ourselves checked out making sure we had received all of our inoculations and vaccines before we were to go aboard the ship that was to take us to the United States. The ship, as they called it, was a U.S. converted battleship named "The General Harry Taylor." Some of the GIs that were also passengers called it a "tub." It was not very large. We started to board in the early afternoon.

All GIs including my husband and many other wives' husbands had to go below and stay in military quarters. The wives had cabins. Some had six bunks in them which meant six women were to share one cabin. We could only see our husbands so many hours per day and up on deck only. Those were the rules as told to us before boarding.

As we all stood on deck and waited for the ship to pull out of the harbor, a military band appeared and played some tunes of goodbyes, the last one being the famous: "Auf Wiedersehen" They were playing it as the ship was pulling up anchor and started pulling away from land. Lots of the girls started crying and waving back to the people on land who were also waving. One of the girls was really having a good cry. Then she said: "When I get to New York, I am going back home." I sort of had to laugh and then I said, "Wouldn't it be much easier to get off here instead of going all of the way to New York first?" She sort of looked at me amazed, then saying between gasps, "But I want to see the Statue of Liberty first." I replied: "Oh, I see. Okay then." So much for that.

I was told where my cabin was and I proceeded to go there, and, yes, I shared it with five more women. There were six of us in all. Three of them were pregnant so they got to sleep on the bottom cot; the rest of us on top. The captain welcomed us and gave us advice as to what to do in order not to become sea sick and to have an enjoyable trip as possible. It would last about ten days. He told us to try and eat our three meals each day and get plenty of fresh air up on deck. There would be movies shown in the evenings that the wives could go see with their husbands, but the husbands were not allowed to walk their wives back to their cabins. They had to return to their quarters below. The only other time they could see each other was on deck in the afternoon from 2 to 4. "Sounds very romantic" someone said out loud. The captain just smiled and said "We have to abide by the rules."

One afternoon when Jim and I could see each other they announced that there was a small gift shop on the ship and couples were encouraged to visit it if they wished to do so. So, Jim and I went and looked around. They had several nice things, some jewelry, perfumes, candies, magazines. I saw a pretty blue beaded necklace with matching earrings that just caught my eye. Jim asked me if I would like having them. I smiled and said "It is a pretty set but it might cost too much money." He said "No, it is not that much and you are worth it." I thanked him and hugged his neck.

On returning to my cabin to dress for dinner I found three very sick women lying on their cots.

They were all vomiting into their paper bags that were provided for such times. It was the three pregnant ones. I felt sorry for them and asked if there was anything I could do or get them. They shook their heads and waved me off with their hand. It was to let me know that they wanted to be left alone. I understood and honestly did not want to be there around all of this smelly vomiting. I went into the bathroom, cleaned up, put my clothes on and got out of there.

CHAPTER XVII

ALMOST RAPED

I went to dinner with the other two girls and then met Jim to go see a movie. They were showing: "How Green Was My Valley." The other two girls from the cabin did not go to the movie that night. One did not feel too great and the other had already seen it. So, after the movie, I had to walk back to my cabin alone. Jim headed downstairs after kissing me good night, and I started to proceed down the dimly lit hallway to go to my cabin. All of a sudden, one of those heavy metal doors opened and a tall and big GI dressed in fatigues put one arm from behind me close to my neck and his other one behind my waist. He tried to pull me inside whatever room that was. I tried to scream and struggled as he pulled me close to the inside when suddenly out of nowhere there appeared another GI. He was young and looked to be of Hispanic heritage. He pulled me out of the big GI's arm and hit him in the face with his fist. The next thing we were all in front of the captain. I was so shook up I was crying. I realized the guy was trying to rape me. Jim was also called. The guy was locked up in the lower level of the ship in a special secured room until we were to arrive in New York. The captain told Jim he could press charges against him then and have him arrested. We both thanked the nice Hispanic

GI for having come to my rescue, saving me from something that could have turned out very tragic.

The next morning an announcement was made that the ship had to turn back and pick up a man from a Puerto Rican fishing boat. He was having an appendix attack and needed an appendectomy. They did not have a doctor on board. We did, so we met the large fishing vessel. He lowered the doctor from our ship into a lifeboat which was then lowered into the waters. A ladder was dropped from the vessel on which our doctor climbed up on. He examined the fisherman then helped getting him down into the life boat that returned back to our ship which had been anchored. The sick man was operated on and kept several hours until he was in the clear. They returned him this time on a stretcher. They pulled him up to the fishing vessel after giving him pain meds and antibiotics. He was released. It cost us more than one day, almost two, to get to our destination.

I did not get seasick on my voyage to America, but I became terribly sunburned, especially on my lower legs. I did what the Captain had said do. I ate all of my meals and got lots of fresh air. What I did not realize was how easy it is to get sun and wind burned. I would sit in one of the lawn chairs and enjoy he cool wind and warm sun blowing over my body. I wore a pair of capris and rolled the legs up to my knees. Bad choice! My legs got to be in bad shape. The doctor rubbed some kind of special ointment on my legs that felt nice and cool, but it hurt from the touch.

One morning close to noon there was excitement among all of the passengers. Everybody seemed to want to go on deck, myself included, to see what all of the excitement was about. There she was, that beautiful lady in the harbor. The Statute of Liberty. What a sight! I became so overwhelmed at her sight that I started crying. I finally have arrived at My Destination, and she was the first sight anyone would see that had the chance to come to this great country. We started packing up our belongings into suitcases. They had to be taken on deck. From there, they would be loaded onto buses that would take us to our hotel where we had to stay for another week while Jim was being released out of the Army, and we would fly on to Tennessee.

The man that attacked me several days ago was brought up on deck to the Captain's office, and Jim had to go in there in order to press charges against him and sign papers that would notify the authorities. They were to pick him up on board in New York, from there to a prison. I did not go in there with Jim. I could not stand to face this man. The fear and horror that I felt that night when he tried to pull me into that room all came back. I waited outside in a small sitting area. Finally, as the door opened and the man reached over and shook Jim's hand saying, "Thank you so much. You have no idea how I appreciate you not pressing charges against me!" I stood with wide eyes and an open mouth. I could not believe what I was seeing and hearing. Did my husband really just shake a man's hand that tried to rape or even kill me? Jim grabbed me by the arm and walked me over to a place where no one stood. We were almost ready to dock. He said, "You know honey, I just could not press charges against him. He told me that he had a wife and five kids waiting for him as soon as he got off the ship and it would ruin the rest of his life." I replied, "But it was so wrong, what he did. He should be punished. He may do this again to another woman." His reply was "Let's just forget it and put it behind us." Somehow, this did something to me. My feelings of wondering did my husband respect someone like that more than me. I did not say another word. What good would it have done any way? He had made up his mind. It was done, but somehow I felt insecure, a bit afraid, and very disrespected. I guess I felt like I had no one in my corner. The Captain of the ship also came out of the room, and as he walked past us I felt like he glanced at me with a sort of pity in his eyes, or maybe it was just my imagination.

We were getting off the ship and proceeded to some parked military transportation buses. When each bus was fully loaded it pulled out and headed towards the inner city of New York. I looked out the window and thought I am now on American soil. Naturally, I was very curious and looked at everything and anything that caught my eyes.

Someone exclaimed "This is the Bronx!" Another replied, "Yea, it is sort of the slum part of the city," and at that time it did look rather dirty. Trash was all over the streets, lots of people and children, some did not look very clean. I was really a bit disappointed seeing all of this, because where I came from it was clean. The streets were always swept and no one was throwing trash on the ground. I thought to myself, gosh, I hope the rest of America does not look like that because if it does then I do not think I care to live here! But, it got better. As we started turning the streets we were headed to Manhattan, then the St. George Hotel. That was to be our home for about one week, married, military only. The rest were to stay on base until their discharge from the military became final. The rest were being shipped to other bases in the U.S. Jim had to report to the base each day and stay there pretty much all day. Therefore, I was pretty much on my own all day. I hung out with some of the other wives. We went shopping and just sort of walked around in the city. In the evenings we would all get together, get on the subway and just go all over. We went to visit Coney Island one afternoon. That is when it was still open. Later, it became closed down for many years to come. There were about six of us, three couples. We had a great time getting on some of the rides, also attending some of the side shows.

I was amazed. There was actually an African lady that had three or four live snakes hanging around her neck. All the while she was dancing to the rhythm of some bongo drums. I was fascinated for I had never seen anything of that sort. Then, one evening we visited the Empire State Building. It was absolutely breathtaking. I can still feel the strong winds blowing as we briefly walked out onto the open deck and getting a look at all of the high-rise buildings. Wow, what a huge and amazing city with its millions of lights. I had never imagined it would be this big.

CHAPTER XVIII

NEW YORK

I really got to liking New York. The hotel in which we stayed was comfortable and very nice. I grew and lived most of my life in the city so New York was very enjoyable, all of the shops with the beautiful clothes and shoes. I sort of went crazy and bought four new dresses with shoes to match and handbags as well. I came to realize that I needed to purchase another suitcase for all of the newly acquired wardrobe, so I found a small store that sold luggage. I explained to the clerk what all I had to put in and he suggested a certain piece of the right size that would hold everything, then he sort of looked at me questioningly and asked "and just where are you traveling to young lady?" I replied, in my broken English, "Oh, I go to Tennessee." He laughed and said "Have you ever been there?" I shook my head, no, grinning. He said, "You know, they live in shacks, wear overalls, go barefoot and they smoke funny corncob pipes. They sit around and drink moonshine all day. My mouth flew open and I stared at him in disbelief. I thought, if this is true, what did I get myself into? He seemed to get a big kick out of picking on me. I paid for my new piece of luggage and walked back to the hotel. I was excited getting to pack all of my new clothes up for our upcoming trip to Tennessee.

Jim was being delayed on base that evening. I started to get hungry and proceeded to order some food from the restaurant inside the hotel and have it brought to our room. Perhaps by the time it was prepared and brought to our room Jim would be here to eat with me, so I picked up the phone and ordered two minute steaks with fries, a salad, rolls and two cokes. I told them to add the charges to our room. They said that was fine. After about 20 minutes or so there was a knock on the door. I opened the door and a waiter pushing a cart with our ordered food entered. After I told him "Come in, please," he rolled the cart to the center of the room and I politely thanked him. He nodded his head but just kept on standing there. I asked him in my broken English "You need wagon now?" He said, "No, when you finish, put it outside the door." I said, "Okay, thank you." So, he still stood there. I looked at him very curiously as to say why are you just standing there, when suddenly he walked towards the door, then turned around with a sarcastic look on his face and said, "Thanks for the tip!" I replied, "You are welcome." He hastily went out of the door almost slamming it. I was puzzled. Shortly after, Jim came. I told him about the incident and the strange behavior of the waiter that brought our food to the room. Jim was smiling. He said, "Well, did you give him a tip." I said, "What is a tip?" He said, "Honey, you were supposed to give him money." I said, "But I told them to put it on our bill." He said, "No, he wanted extra money for bringing the food up to the room, and when he told you 'Thanks for the tip' and you said 'You are welcome' that upset him." "Oh, I thought, he thanked me for ordering the food. That is way I said you are welcome." That little encounter really made me feel bad. I thought I really need to learn his language and all of the strange words or I would get in all kinds of trouble.

We packed up all of our clothes and other belongings to get ready for the next day when we were to take a mid-morning flight that was to take us to our final destination, Nashville, Tennessee. Jim called his parents and told them what time our plane would land so they could be at the airport to pick us up. I cannot describe how nervous and uneasy I felt that morning when I awakened. I had never been on nor flown on an airplane before. I was to fly to some state called Tennessee where I would be surrounded by lots of people called hillbillies going around barefoot, smoking corncob pipes and living in shacks. I was to meet my inlaws for the very first time. Were they going to be Tennessee hillbillies? I tried to calm myself down. Jim had told me his parents lived on a nice farm, the countryside was beautiful, and his Dad raised tobacco. Okay, the taxi came. Our luggage was being loaded into the trunk. We took a seat in the rear and headed towards the airport. Jim took my hand and smiled. He said, "You know, it feels good being a free man again and do whatever one wants to do. I can go fishing, hunting whenever I please. I don't have to ask Uncle Sam when I can or can't go. "You have to ask your Uncle Sam if you can go do something. Will he be at the airport, too? Nothing I said or heard seemed to make much sense. Jim just laughed. Then, he explained the best he could who Uncle Sam was and what it meant. So much for the Uncle Sam. Here was the airport, and it would be no time before we were to board this big metal bird that was going to climb up to the sky and fly us to my new home. Oh me, I was having a terrible attack of butterflies rumbling around in my stomach. We checked in our luggage then went through the line to board our plane. I looked at Jim. "You have flown before, how is it?" He smiled and said "It will be just fine, and we will be there in no time, a couple of hours, that is all."

We were seated. Jim let me sit by the window. That was okay. I did want a good look out, especially when the State of Tennessee would come in sight. I would be checking out those hills and, of course, if I could see any of the people that lived there. I could not believe how excited I felt when the plane started to taxi down the runway real slow. Then, as it turned on to another long runway the speed picked up tremendously. I felt a rush of adrenaline as the plane left the ground and started climbing. I loved it and do until this day. There is something very intense and exciting in that moment. The stewardess was giving her routine instruction for any emergency that might arise. I decided that I actually love to fly and I remembered that this is all what I really wanted to become was a flight stewardess.

CHAPTER XIX

TENNESSEE AT LAST

Jim was right. We landed in a couple of hours. While getting our luggage, Jim spotted his Dad. He ran up to him and they hugged. I sort of stood to the side, then Jim took me by the arm and said to his Dad, "Here is your new daughter." Dewey, that was his name, smiled and held his arms out to give me a big hug. He said, "Welcome." I thanked him. He seemed like a sweet man and I immediately took a liking to him. Then, he told Jim, "She sure is pretty." I smiled and thanked him once more.

After we got our luggage, we headed towards the exit and where the car was parked. Jim's Mom, Virgie Mae, as she was called, got out and came over. She grabbed Jim and hugged him, all the while crying and laughing at the same time. I am sure she had missed him lots on his three-year absence in the military. He only came home once on a furlough. After an emotional welcome, I was introduced and hugged by his Mom. She was a rather small petite woman with brown hair and spunky brown eyes. Jim had told me back in Germany that his grandparents on both sides were part British and Cherokee Indian Heritage. It really showed up in his mother and maternal grandmother's appearance. The Cherokee side was strongly portrayed. On his father's side it showed up more so in his grandfather. We did not say a whole lot until after we got the luggage loaded. We got into the car and I got to see Nashville for the very first time. Was I ever so relieved not seeing all those barefooted hillbillies running around. Actually, everybody looked just as normal as they did anywhere else in the world. I was very busy looking out the window while Jim was very busy talking to his parents about all sorts of things. I understood that they were going to have lots of people come over that evening to see Jim and meet his new wife.

We were now headed north leaving Nashville and driving into a small town called Millersville. Jim's Dad pulled up in front of a small diner. It was operated by an elderly lady named Pauline. She cooked up the food most of the time herself. After being introduced once more we were seated and ordered four hamburger platters with fries and coke. Pauline sat with us while we ate. It tasted really good. Besides, Jim and I were pretty hungry. I noticed that Pauline had a diamond ring of some sort on every finger on both of her hands. She saw me looking at all of those rings. Laughing, she held her hands up and said, "Honey, I have been married seven times and I always wanted a diamond ring on each finger. I had to buy three on my own because I ran out of men. I almost forgot to swallow my food and had to grab my coke to wash it down in order that I would not choke laughing.

After eating and saying goodbye to Pauline, we got back into Dewey's 1949 Chevrolet and headed up the ridge towards Greenbrier. I had to admire the countryside around us and on each side of the road. Tennessee sure is a beautiful place. Those were my thoughts. We rode about ten minutes when we turned off left on some country road. There were not many houses, one here, one there, and lots of farmland. Everything seemed to be so far apart, and I could not believe the wide open spaces. It was quite different from where I came from. We turned onto another road and Jim's mom said we are almost there. This is the road we live on. I nodded and smiled at her. Up the road on the left appeared a beautiful, large, white farmhouse. That must be it, I thought. Jim had told me that they lived on a real nice farm, but to my surprise they did not stop at the pretty white farmhouse. That very house, I found out later belonged to the people that owned the farm. Jim's Dad was a crop sharer, as they called it, and lived with his wife in a small wood-framed house. It had a large kitchen, two bedrooms, living room, and a large front porch, a small back porch with a well behind it and a little further away was an outhouse – toilet. The house in which they lived in belonged to the owners of the farm. I never asked whether or not Dewey and Virgie Mae had to pay any rent or if they got to live there for free. I also noticed that "Jim" was called "James" by his parents and everyone else around that was related or knew him otherwise. Eventually, I, too, started to call him James, for if I spoke to anyone about Jim they would look at me and say "You mean James?" I guess whenever he entered the military someone decided to change James into Jim. I never really found out. We pulled up to the house and unloaded our suitcases with James's Dad's help. We entered the small country house and I was impressed how neat and clean everything looked. The furniture seemed to be antique, but none of it was fancy. James's Mom showed me the bedroom. It was pretty large, furnished with a double bed, dresser, chest of drawers and nightstand. There was a wardrobe to hang our clothes and a round table in front of the window with a chair at the side. I loved the antique lamp that sat on top of the table. Our suitcases were taken to our bedroom, but James's parents told us to come and sat down and take a rest before we started our unpacking. Besides, we were told there were several relatives and friends that wanted to stop by to see him and meet his new bride.

CHAPTER XX

SOMEWHAT DIFFERENT

James's Dad walked over to a drawer and pulled out a white envelope. He came over and handed it to me. This came for you. I think it is a letter from your folks in Germany. I cannot tell anyone how overwhelmed I became when I reached up for the letter. Just then, I realized how much I missed my parents and all that I left behind. I had come to a world so very different from where I came from. It was not that I did not like it. It was just all so new and different. I also knew that I was a very long way away from my home, but, of course, this was my home now and this is where I chose to live.

I walked into the large kitchen. It, too, was very bright and neat. In the center was a large Formica-top table with chrome legs surrounded by six yellow plastic seated chairs. In one corner was an electric stove, sort of caddy-cornered. Then, there was a large, old fashioned wood-burning cooking stove. Several white metal cabinets lined one wall, a refrigerator at the opposite side, then a stand on which sat a bucket that contained water drawn from a well outside. On its side hung a ladle. I noticed from time to time everyone just seemed to walk up to it, grab the ladle, dip it in the water and get a drink.

I was told that I could call my new in laws Mom and Dad if I wished to do so. I thought, well, my Mom and Dad are so far away so they would be my husband's parents and someday our children's grandparents. I accepted their offer, gave them a hug and called them Mom and Dad. I excused myself and went out on the porch. I took a seat on the wooden swing and started to read my letter. I loved each and every word in it. After all, it came from two people that meant so much but were so far away. Mom wrote that she was really showing now and felt awkward at times getting around. She was now six months pregnant and had three more to go. She and Dad wrote about my grandparents and what other family and friends were doing. They said they really missed me and wanted me to write as much as I could.

I had just finished reading my letter when a couple of cars pulled in the driveway, then another and another. I stepped back inside the house and sat down on the couch next to James. He then jumped up and went to the door greeting cousins, aunts, uncles and friends. Everyone seemed excited and did lots of talking. Then, the attention turned towards me. I was introduced to so many people with names, some I had never heard of. James took off outside with a couple of his male cousins. The rest sat wherever there was room to sit. Chairs were pulled in from the kitchen and bedrooms. Everyone was talking. Somehow, I could feel lots of eyes staring at me, but they really did not speak to me directly. I felt like someone had just dropped me off in the middle of something very strange and I felt so uneasy and alone. I got up and walked to the door. I saw James being involved in some conversation about one of his cousin's cars for the hood of the car was raised up and they had their heads stuck down looking at the inside – for what, I had no clue. Maybe it was selfish of me, but I somehow felt that he needed to be by my side and not having left me with all of these people that just seemed to look at me very curiously as if I had come from out of space. Everyone knew that I did not speak the language too well and that I had quite an accent. Being plain country people, maybe they felt strange being around me as well. I excused myself and walked into the kitchen where a backdoor led to behind the house. No one was around except for a couple of beagle hounds, chickens and me. I noticed a trail that led up towards a wooded area so I just started walking that way until the house was no longer in sight and I was now all alone. Oh, how alone I felt at the moment. I looked at the beautiful sunset. Then I sat down in the grass and tried to sort out things in my head. Was I not supposed to be really happy and in love, but I felt that James had just sort of dropped me off since we arrived. He did not seem to have any time nor concern for me. Now, I really needed him to be close and comfort me. I was so alone in a strange new country. All at once I lay down in the grass and cried my heart out. Oh, how I cried and then cried some more. Then, I tried to calm myself down and go back. I had to be brave. I could not fall apart. I could not let my parents know how homesick I was for they would have worried themselves something terrible, especially when my Mom was expecting a baby. No, I could never let them know. I walked back towards the house and I saw James walking up saying "Where have you been? We have company. My sister and Ken and the two little girls just arrived." I swallowed and said "Oh, I just wanted to walk up to the woods. I guess it was kind of silly what I did, but I just had to get away from all of those people who just seemed to stare at me." I don't think he was too happy with my behavior and neither was I with his.

CHAPTER XXI

STRANGE CUSTOMS

ome of the people that came earlier started to leave. I met his sister Mary, nieces Debbie and Cathy, and, of course, Ken, whom I had already met. Ken smiled and gave me a big hug. Mary looked at me and said "Hi Sis. Ken told me how pretty you were. You are indeed." I smiled, thanked her and proceeded to hug the little girls. Debbie, the oldest, almost three, came right up to me for hugs, but the little one, Cathy, would have nothing to do with me. One of James' uncles called her "sour puss" for she hardly ever smiled whereas Debbie seemed to smile nonstop. It felt good seeing Ken again. He was someone familiar that I had met back in Germany, but I could tell that Mary was the jealous type and she made no secret about it. As a matter of fact, later, after we all ate dinner and I went to our bedroom to hang up some clothes, Mary followed me and lay across the bed watching me hang up my clothes that I unpacked from the suitcase. Suddenly, out of the clear blue sky, she said, "I don't like any woman messing around with Ken." I was shocked and angry at the same time. I thought to myself what a nice welcome she is giving me. Instead, I looked at her straight in the eyes and all I said, "I married your brother and I don't want your husband." I guess she could tell that I was annoyed with her comment and that she should have kept it to herself. Then, she tried to be really nice and said, "I am going to give you and James a shower." This time I really whirled around and told her, "Oh no, you are not. I am clean. I took a shower in New York this morning. I thought if that is a custom here and the family wants to give me a shower, well I am just going back home! I have never seen a woman laughing as hard as she did. I thought she was going to roll off the bed, tears of laughter coming down from her eyes. I was beginning to doubt her sanity. When she finally caught her breath, she started to explain to me that she was talking about a gift shower. I had no clue about none of these things. All I understood when she first talked about it was that she wanted to wash us down from head to toe. Not me, not in any one's wildest dreams. We seemed to get along pretty well after we understood where each one was coming from.

I started to understand people more and more and was able to communicate pretty well. James had found a job. It was the construction of the Ford Glass Plant that was being built in Nashville. I was glad for we wanted to save up money and get an apartment in Nashville. We would not live forever with his parents. I also found out that I, too, had become pregnant, my very first month in the U.S. I did not feel very good and had lots of morning sickness. Soon, we found a furnished one bedroom apartment in East Nashville. It was located upstairs in a private family home with the owners living downstairs. It was the month of June now and the temperature became pretty warm. It was hot in that upstairs apartment having only a window fan for the means of cooling. I really enjoyed living in a place of our own, even if it meant not having our own furniture. We had lots of nice dishes, figurines, towels and linens that helped to give the place a cozy and homey look. I enjoyed doing my own cooking. It was a mixture of German, which I had learned from my Mom, and some newly learned skills I had acquired from my mother-in-law called "Southern country cooking." James said he liked my cooking, and that was good.

After our apartment was all neat and I was caught up with laundry, cooking and so on, I started to get bored and decided one morning to catch a city bus which stopped down by the corner of our street. I felt that I, too, should try and find a job to contribute to our income, especially now that a baby was on the way. I paid the driver and took a seat. The bus kept making a few more stops until it pulled up at a corner up town. I saw that all kinds of stores were located on each side of the street. I looked up at the street sign. It said Second Avenue. I noticed a large store on my right hand side. It said Dollar Store. I decided just to walk in. I walked up to a young brown-haired woman and told her my name and that I was looking for a job. She smiled and said, "My name is Pat. Come with me." We walked towards the back of the store where an older gentleman was talking to another young employee. Pat introduced me to him saying "Mr, Kassman. He is the boss and he is in charge of hiring the help." He was an older man, perhaps in his mid sixties. He had no hair and wore dark horn-rimmed eyeglasses, but he smiled and shook my hand saying "So, you are a little German girl. Well, I too, am of German heritage. My parents were immigrants but I was born here. He asked about what my qualifications consisted of, so I told him that I had finished my education in Germany and that I had completed my typing, shorthand and bookkeeping skills. In other words, I was able to do secretarial work. He looked at me sideways, then he replied, "Well, you are really over qualified for the kind of job that I have to offer you. It is keeping the shelves and the tables stocked and helping customers find things." I said, "Oh, I will be glad to do that." I knew that I was still pretty handicapped with my English language and would not probably be able to handle an office job at present. This job here would be great for a start. He said "It pays one dollar per hour and I can give you thirty hours a week." I was so happy. The very first store that I had walked into and I had a job. Mr. Kassman asked if I could start the next day. I told him I would be there. He wanted me to come in around 10 and work until 4 in the afternoon. I shook his hand and said "Thank you, sir. I will be here." I thanked Pat for her help and then I left. I was so excited I wanted to get back home and cook dinner before James got off from his job.

CHAPTER XXII

LOST IN NASHVILLE

I walked back to the same corner and when the bus pulled up I got on, paid my fee, and had a seat. All I could think about was that I have a job and I will be making some money to start buying baby clothes. It seemed that I was riding on this bus quite a bit longer than I did before. As I started looking out the window I did not see anything that looked very familiar, not at all. Oh, where was I supposed to get off? Did I even get on the right bus? Panic suddenly filled my whole mind and body. The driver was of no help. He did not know the street where I lived. I think I wound up in a totally different part of town. Panic and worried of being lost, I got off at the next stop. After the bus pulled off and drove away, I stood at the edge of the sidewalk thinking what I could do. I did not know anybody in this town. I had no one I could call. I saw a police car coming down the street so I stepped off the sidewalk and started to wave him down. Naturally, he pulled over and got out. I explained my situation to him and that I did not know how I was going to get back home. The officer was really nice, but I could tell that he really tried hard to keep from bursting out in a big laugh. He opened the car door and told me to have a seat in the rear, of course. He said he knew where I lived and it was in the East part of town. I was in West Nashville. The officer radioed in and then we were on our way. I could not believe I had gotten myself in this embarrassing situation. I was so nervous and upset. The officer wanted to know my house number where I lived. I could not even think of it. I told him I would recognize the house, so he slowly drove up the street. When I saw the house where our apartment was upstairs, I said, "There it is." Laughingly, he said, "Are you sure little lady." I said, "Yes, that is it. How much do I owe you?" He said, "You do not owe me a thing. Just promise me that you learn which bus you have to catch that brings you back home safe, and you did the right thing by asking the law for help." I said, "Oh, thank you so very much." I shook his hand and headed up to our apartment. What a day this turned out to be! I started to fix dinner when James came in. I told him about my job and what all had happened. He just shook his head, then he laughed. I had to laugh with him. It was really all very funny then. He said you can catch the bus in the morning, but I will pick you up when I get off work. He got off at 3:30, so that would work out just great for him to pick me up at my job at 4 when I got off.

That evening after we had finished dinner, Mary and Ken stopped by to see us. They brought another couple along with them and told us that they were their best friends. They, too, lived in East Nashville, not far from where we lived. They were David and Jo Ann Bragg. They seemed real nice, especially Jo Ann. She was also very pretty. She had short dark hair and beautiful blue eyes. They sparkled when she smiled. She spoke to me as I was her best friend, and I immediately took a liking to her. Mary said, "She is my best friend." I said, "I can see that can very easily happen with a very nice young lady such as she is.!" Jo Ann smiled and winked at me. She and I became best friends and are still to this day very close. Her husband, David, was more of a quiet type guy. He did not talk very much. He did, however, mention that he, too, had just gotten back from Germany where he had served in the military and that he had really liked Germany. I was glad to have met some nice people that lived in our area. We promised to get back together again real soon.

The next day I got up and got James off to his job. Afterwards, I made up the bed, straightened the apartment up and then got ready for work. I was excited and wondered what all I would be doing on my first day. I walked down to the corner again and caught the bus. I knew where I had to get off and I did not have a problem finding the store that I was to go to work in. Pat greeted me by giving me a hug. She said, "Come, I will show you the back room. We have a place where you can put your handbag and a refrigerator where we keep our drinks and lunches. Then, she trained me, showing me how to fold and stack towels on a table, coordinating the colors, sizes, etc. It was all very easy and I did not have any problems. I liked my coworkers and my boss as well. The first day went by pretty fast. It was not long until I waited outside in front of the store for my ride. James pulled up in our blue and white 1954 Ford. It was his first car ever and he enjoyed driving it. I did not have a driver's license yet. I had to wait until I was 18.

Summer was really hot. I started drinking lots of ice cold cokes thinking it would keep me cool. Instead, I wound up a very sick girl. I started running a temperature and had terrible back pains. I got so sick I could not get out of bed. When James came home that afternoon he helped me pack up a few things and we headed to the country to stay with his parents until I got well. Besides, Dr. Hirsch, who was also my doctor, was to see me the next morning. He, too, lived in the country. His Dad drove me to see Dr. Hirsch since James had to go to work. Dr. Hirsch and his wife (She was an R.N. and worked as his assistant) were real nice people. He examined me and said that I had a terrible kidney infection, drinking six to eight cokes each day, not being used to the intense hot Tennessee climate and being pregnant took its toll on my health. He said he did not want me standing on my feet all day and I should have somebody with me to help take care of me. So, the decision was made. We were going to move back in with his parents until later and we could get a nice apartment that would not be so hot such as this one had been. I was now really sick, trying to deal with morning sickness, getting over a kidney infection, and living in someone else's home again. It seemed to have affected our relationship. When James was not working he would go off evenings to ball games and just hanging out with some of his cousins and friends. I stayed there with his parents. We would go and visit both grandparents or stop at one of the other many relative's houses, then come back home.

I lived each day for the arrival of the mail. I got so bored and not having much of anything to do, so I went for a walk. I strolled down the country road and it seemed to clear my mind. I felt good and I just wanted to keep on walking. I decided to walk down to the hollow where James' paternal grandparents lived. I had become sort of close to them. They were the sweetest people. James and Mary called them Mamie and Pa. They wanted me to call them that as well. Mamie used to bake me yellow cakes with caramel icing. It was so good. She was a great cook. She always gave me a hug and Pa loved to sit and talk for hours, and he made no secret as to how much he loved all the ladies. His favorite thing to do was to reach down to his toes with his hands, then kicking up his legs, then exclaiming "Shucks, I am just like a young man." Mamie, in turn, would fuss at him. Sometimes she would say, "You are just an old fool." They would fuss to no end sometime, but it was also very comical. They were sitting in their rocking chairs when I walked up to the house. Naturally, they were both surprised and at the same time very happy to see me. I got my usual hugs from both, and after I was given a cool glass of grape Kool Aid, I sat down and had a real nice visit. Neither of them could say my name right, so she called me "Helen." He called me "Helden." It was so funny. They had their youngest son Roy nicknamed and called him Dinkie living with them. He never was married, but he, too, was real nice. He liked visiting the honky tonks on weekends and Mamie and Pa used to get on to him all of the time. They all three always tried to talk at the same time. Then, they would start fussing at one another. They were truly fun to watch.

I enjoyed my afternoon and time got away from me. That is when James' car pulled up. He got out and walked over towards me just yelling, asking what did I mean just taking off walking and not telling anyone where I was going. That made me very angry. I felt like I was a little child being gotten on to by her daddy. At the same time I was embarrassed because of the way he yelled at me in front of his uncle and grandparents. They were startled over his outburst and they tried taking up for me by saying, "Now James, you should not be talking to her like that. She did not do anything wrong. She just came to visit us and we love having her." He said, "Hell. She walked two damn miles. I told him I used to walk more than that in Germany. Walking is good exercise. He gave all of us a dirty look and turned and walked to his car, got in it and took off with gravel flying every which way. I could not believe that he could get that angry because I went to visit his grandparents. Then, to top it all, just leaving without me. Mamie came over and hugged me. She could see that I was upset and close to tears. She said, "You eat super with us, then we will get somebody to take you home." I said, "That is okay. I can walk but thank you anyway." She fixed some dinner and I ate with them. Somehow, I always felt good and comforted in their presence. We had just finished eating when Dewey and Virgie Mae pulled up in their 49 Chevy. They did not look too happy either. Mom said, "You should not have walked off two miles and you pregnant." I said, "I just started walking and decided after I left the house to come down here for a visit. What is wrong with that? I am a grown woman. Why is everybody so upset because I took a walk and visited the grandparents? Oh, and where is James? Why didn't he come to get me? He left here mad and embarrassed me." She answered, "He left. He was upset. That is why Dewey and I came to get you." "Fine, I said. First, I am going to help Mamie with the dinner dishes. She said, "Oh no Helen, you go on. Dinkie is going to do them." I hugged all three and thanked them for dinner and showing me so much kindness. I also told them that I would be back. I got in the backseat and we headed towards the house. James was gone. I asked if they knew where he went, but they told me no, they didn't. He just left. I sat in the living room with them until 9 p.m. Then, I said I did not feel too good and I was tired, so I went to our room and went to bed. I could not sleep. Instead, I cried, cried and cried. I felt like I was the unhappiest girl in the world. James came home around 2:30 a.m. I could smell alcohol. I did not say a word, but I could not sleep the rest of the night. I felt sharp pains in my back when I got up the next morning and when I used the pot, which we used during the night, there was blood. She said, "You probably have a kidney infection." James, too, got up and came to the kitchen for breakfast. His Dad did not look very happy and gave him a talk about going off the way he did the night before and leaving me alone. He said, "You brought this girl to this country. She is your wife and is expecting your baby. You are not going to treat her this way, especially not in this house under our roof." He never answered his Dad. He just sort of dropped his head and mumbled an "I'm sorry" towards me.

I did have some good times while living in the country. James' dad came in from the fields in early afternoons. He always made popcorn for us and then we would watch TV together. He would make the popcorn in a large pot with a lid on the electric stove that sat cattycornered in the kitchen. One day he was late getting in from the fields so I decided to make the popcorn myself. I had never "popped" popcorn before, so after I had turned on the burner and added the cooking oil, I was curious how those little kernels could transform into big white puffs of corn so I left the top off of the pot and watched them. It wasn't long before the little kernels began popping, all at the same time. Popcorn began flying everywhere. I was afraid to put the lid on the pot and ran into the living room with popcorn flying about behind me. It was about that time when the kitchen door opened and in walked Dad. His eyes widened at the scene and then he realized what had happened. He went to the stove, removed the cooking pot and turned the burner off. He then burst out in laughter. We both swept up the scattered popcorn and cleaned up my mess. From then on I left the popcorn making to him.

CHAPTER XXIII

PAINFUL TIMES

I did not feel good the rest of the day and not that night. I felt back pain and pressure in my stomach and still lost blood. I was so young and had no clue what was happening. No one else seemed to pay any attention either. The next day I got so sick and was in so much pain I could not get out of bed. I felt like I was running a fever. I told James to drive down to the farmhouse and call Dr. Hirsch. They did not have a phone of their own during that time. He went and called. An hour later Dr. and Mrs. Hirsch pulled up in their car and came into the house. The doctor came straight to my bed and looked at me. He touched my stomach, going all over the area, mashing lightly, then using the stethoscope listening for a while. He said, "There is no time to take this girl to the hospital. Her baby is dead and needs to be delivered now. Why was she not brought to see me earlier. You folks best get on your knees and pray for her life is hanging on a very fine thread." Then, he gave his wife orders and told James and his Mom to hold me down. They had to take my baby then and there, and I was told that it had been dead inside of me for two days and I would have died. I felt so sad and empty at the same time. Dr. Hirsch and his wife took the baby with them. It was baptized, put in a small box and buried on their farm. He told me when I came to his office for a recheck not to get pregnant for at least one year.

Life went on. We still lived in the country. James' job with the construction came to an end, so now he was trying to find a new job. His mom also started back to work. She was usually off for a couple of months during the summer before going back to the Standard Candy Company where she worked and had for years. I stayed at the house, pretty much by myself and did some work there. I also wrote lots of letters to my friends and family. Mom's time was getting close to have the baby, so I was getting anxious and excited waiting for the news. Meanwhile, I had two little friends that used to come and visit me. They were 11-year-old twins and distant cousins of James' named Reid and Teddy Wayne. I should state that by now I had started to smoke a little. I did not inhale the smoke. I just sort of puffed on the cigarette. Well, Reid and Teddy asked me one time if I would let them have a cigarette. They told me that they ran out. I said, "Oh no. Don't tell me you both already smoke?" Two blond haired, blue-eyed boys grinned and replied,"Oh, just now and then, but please do not tell anyone." "Hum," I said. "I will not tell, but you two need to quit smoking. You are too young." I also told them that I would not give them another one. So, one day when James rode with his cousin, they both went for job interviews. I took the car to drive down the road to a small country store to pick up something I needed to make a dessert. Reid and Teddy rode with me. I was not a very experienced driver then, and when I cut my wheel too short I wound up in a ditch and could not get out. Reid and Teddy volunteered to go across the road to a neighboring farmer and let him pull us out. The nice man did just that. We thanked him and I also told him not to tell anyone. He promised he wouldn't. Now, the twins were snickering, laughing and teasing me to no end. "Helga drove in the ditch" over and over. I finally had enough. I turned around and looked at both. "Now let me tell you right now. If you two just as much as say one word about this, your Momma and Daddy and everyone else will hear about their two smoking little boys!" Their eyes got big and wide and shaking those blond GI Joe haircut heads they said over and over, "Oh no, we promise. We will not tell on you." As far as I know, they never did, and I never told on them either.

James found a job with a trucking company that was in town, so we had hopes of getting to move again real soon. We just needed to have a couple of weeks to save up enough to rent another furnished apartment. Furniture was one thing we did not have. We had a bridal shower given by Mary and that resulted in giving us pretty much everything we needed as far as cooking utensils and small electric appliances. We had all of the other things we brought from Germany.

One day, Charles Swift, the owner of the farm, pulled up in his truck and said, "Helga, come on, get in. You have a phone call at the house. It is your Dad!" I jumped right in and we drove down to his house. His wife, Dean, smiled and said "Hi" and handed me the phone. Oh yes, it was my dear Daddy. How wonderful it was to hear his voice. He asked how I was and felt. Then, he said, "Well, you have a little brother now. He was born last night and we named him Norbert." I was laughing and crying all at the same time. "Oh Daddy, how is Mom." "She is okay. Just a little tired," he said. I wish I could be there and hold him in my arms. Please give him a kiss from his big sister and tell him I love him very much. Give Mom a hug and tell her that I love and miss her and I wish I could be there to help take care of her and the baby. Dad said, "I know, honey. By the way, someone wants to say something." It was my sweet grandfather. "Hallo, Helga," he cried. He told me how much he and my grandma missed me. I said, "Same here." He told me what a beautiful baby my little brother was. He said, "Helga, he has lots of dark hair, beautiful dark blue eyes, and the longest eyelashes that I have ever seen." I said, "Oh, he must be beautiful." We said a few more words. Dad promised to take lots of pictures and send them to me. Then, we hung up. I was so happy and excited I hugged everybody and told them about my beautiful little brother that crossed my path the rest of the day. I told James, "We have to go shopping for Norbert and buy some baby clothes. I want to send him a package." He said, "okay." We did buy several nice outfits including a beautiful light blue snow suit for the coming winter. Winters are cold in Germany. We also put some things in for my Mom and Dad.

A few weeks passed and we had found another apartment in Nashville. This one was really nice and located down stairs. It was completely furnished and consisted of a large living/dining room, large bedroom and bath. Now, the kitchen was rather small. It had a stove, refrigerator, a few wall cabinets, a sink and small counter top, and a table with 2 chairs. It would be enough for us for now. Maybe later we would have another baby and then get a larger place and our own furniture. James seemed to like his job and I enjoyed living in town again in our own place.

It was November now, and I found out that I was expecting another baby. I know I was told to wait a year before becoming pregnant again, but I was very anxious to become a mom. It seemed like everyone around me, including my own Mom, was having babies. I truly longed to hold my own baby in my arms. Dr. Hirsch figured the date to be August 7, 1957 when our baby was due. That meant that my little brother and our baby would be lacking two days, one year apart. Norbert's birthday was August 9·

1956. Wow. Mom and Dad were by now considering to start paperwork and immigrate to the U.S. Also, that thrilled me to no end. I was so excited. They talked about selling out their business, come over here where they would have both of their children and grandchildren around them and make a fresh start once more. During that time it was necessary in order to immigrate to the U.S., one had to have a sponsor that was well established, especially financially, for they had to put up a certain amount of money which had to be deposited into a special account and remain there until the immigrants themselves became established and became of American citizenship after a five-year residency in the U.S. So, my dear friends, Dr. and Mrs. Hirsch willingly agreed to sponsor my parents to come to the U.S. How big and generous that was. The Hirsch's were super nice people. They had even offered to pay for and send me to Vanderbilt to study and become an R.N., but I was always talked out of it. Oh well, that is just the way things were. I knew though that things would get better for me once my parents lived here. At least, I had someone to go to and talk to. I felt so alone all of the time. I had not met many people I could become friends with. They were all his family and his friends. I always felt like I did not belong. The Hirschs were good friends and were willing to help me anyway they could, but I knew they were very busy with all of their patients, two offices and two children of their own – a son, Ray, in the military and a daughter, Claire, in college studying to become a school teacher.

We went to the country every weekend to visit James's parents. He hunted and fished every free time he had. I stayed with his parents or I stayed back at the apartment. I received a letter from home saying that Norbert was very sick with diarrhea. He had gotten dehydrated and had to be put in the hospital, but they said he would probably be alright and get to come home soon. Then, one day my phone rings. It was my Dad. His voice was very shaky and he started crying, while all the time I am saying "What is wrong Daddy? What happened?" He said, "Helga, your little brother died at 3 in the afternoon." It was December 9th. Shortly four months since he was born. I started crying so hard I had to quit talking. James took the phone and talked to my Dad, then I took it back and asked, "Daddy, what happened?" He said that a new nurse had put a baby with diphtheria in the same room with the other babies and four of them died, including Norbert. I thought my heart was going to burst. I had never seen the little angel, but I loved him so and had anticipated so strongly to get to meet and love him, the brother I had always wanted. It was all very hard for me. I could not fly home to be with my parents and attend my little brother's funeral service. As I had mentioned earlier, I, too, was expecting a baby once more and having lost my first one I was strongly advised not to take the trip. All of the emotional part alone was hard for me. All that was left for me to do was praying and writing letters and cards of comfort to my Mom and Dad. I must admit, it was a very sad time for me. There was so much I wanted to do and be there for my parents, but could not.

Spring arrived and with it my 18th birthday. I was now eligible to get my driver's license. I studied all of the rules and regulations in the book. I knew how to drive. I had plenty of practice on those traffic-free country roads while living there. Anyway, I passed my test the very first time that I went to take it. Several people told me that I probably would fail it the first time for some did. I was glad to have gotten it. Now, I, too, would be able to drive our car and go places.

Summer was nearing and the baby in my stomach was growing. I was gaining lots of weight. I loved to eat and

I drank lots of milk. My favorite pastime was sitting in a chair with a carton, one-half gallon, whole milk, with a straw inserted, and I drank and drank and drank until it was empty. On weekends I got to go to the Krystal drive in. I ordered six hamburgers, fries and coke, after which we would drive up the street to the Krispy Kreme Doughnut Shop and buy a dozen doughnuts, which in turn I would attack after getting home with my favorite beverage. You guessed it – one-half gallon of Sealtest milk. So, my so used to be shapely body ballooned to 185 pounds. That is what I weighed when my first-born son, Ronnie, was born in August 7th. He only weighed 6 pounds, 13 ½ ounces, and I had a very hard delivery. It took almost 30 hours to have him, but it was all worth it. I cannot describe the feeling I had when he was laid in my arms the very first time. He opened his beautiful brown eyes and looked at me. I became so overwhelmed that I cried. I kissed him and said, "Hi, my sweet baby. I am your Mommy." Oh, how proud I was to have become a Mom and have a beautiful baby boy. A boy is what we both had hoped for. I had this little person in my life now that I was responsible for and would take care of the very best way I knew how.

We came home and James's mother was to stay with us for a few days. She was to show me how to bathe the baby and care for the small post-umbilical cord that was still attached to the baby's naval. At first, I was afraid to care for this tiny little person, afraid I would somehow hurt him, but even when I gave him his first bath it came all so natural as if I had been doing this all of my life. My Mom and Dad had sent all of Norbert's clothes, his baby crib, baby carriage, all from Germany. Friends of ours that were still in the military but coming back to the U.S. brought those things back for us. It would have cost way too much to send per mail and through customs. Everything was like brand new and in perfect condition.

When Ronnie was a couple of weeks old I took him for a ride down the sidewalks for several blocks each day. He seemed to enjoy the ride. He was a very good baby and cried very little. Now, when his Dad went off hunting or fishing on weekends, I would take Ronnie on rides for hours at a time. I had someone I loved and could take care of. He so filled my lonely hours.

Mom and Dad got a call from the American consulate in Munich. They were being summoned to come for the physical and an interview before being granted a Visa and passport for the USA. Upon their arrival and followed by the interviews with the consulate, he asked them where the child was that was documented in the application. They answered, "We lost him, and he passed away." The consulate asked if they had reported it and did they bring a death certificate. They replied with a "no." My Dad said that my Mom was so torn by grief that they never thought about it having been something very important that needed to be reported. Having been more than eight months, almost nine, since their first application, they had to start their paperwork all over again. So, they went back to Nuremberg and for several months did nothing for meanwhile my dear grandmother became very ill with breast cancer and she died right afterwards. Mom and Dad were very concerned about my Grandaddy. He took his beloved wife's death very hard. She was only 56 when she died. Mom and Dad took my Grandpa on outings with them. He ate most all of his meals with them, and when he didn't he ate with Uncle Robert and Aunt Frieda.

A few months passed and I kept sending pictures home of Ronnie and us. Mom and Dad wished to be around their first grandson and, naturally, they also missed me. Having suffered so many losses, they decided to restart their paper-work for their immigration to the U.S. I was so happy upon hearing the good news. Mom and Dad started to send pretty large amounts of money over. It was deposited into a bank account that was to go towards the purchase of a home whenever they came over. I took care of it for them and deposited all checks upon arrival into their accounts which was listed in my name as well.

Christmas came and it was exciting buying toys for Ronnie. He was 16 months old and talked like a three to four year old. He was only 8 ½ months when he walked and pedaled a tricycle at age one. He was really very advanced for a child his age.

I started to have terrible morning nausea. Smelling bacon cooking or coffee brewing made me gag and rush-ing for a bathroom. One can only imagine what happened next. I could barely start brushing my teeth. Dr. Hirsch confirmed what I had suspected – pregnant. I could expect another baby by mid-September. What would we do? We still lived in a one bedroom furnished apartment. Where would our baby sleep? Still, I was so happy of becom-ing a Mom again. I had a feeling it would be a little girl. Everything was so different, the morning sickness, my shape – all very different.

Mom and Dad kept in close contact with me and informed me how their immigration paper process was developing. They said that it should not be too much lon-ger before they would be coming and for us to go ahead and find a house, put down a down payment and move in. Therefore, every weekend the three of us headed out to the suburbs where nice new homes were being built. After looking at several, we found a nice newly built one that no one had ever lived in. It was a ranch type, light pink brick that sat on a one acre lot with a wooded area behind the house. It consisted of a two-car garage, a large den with fireplace, a built in kitchen with dining area, a large formal dining room, three large bedrooms and one and one-half baths. I called Mom and Dad and told them about the house and how much it cost. They seemed to like the house as I described it to them, and they said "Go ahead and buy it!" They also wanted us to go ahead and move in which meant that we had to buy new furniture. We went to a local furniture store and bought a double bed bedroom suite for us, the first one we ever owned. We bought a couple of twin beds, Western style for Ronnie's room, (They could also be made into bunk beds.), a dresser, night stand and chest of drawers. For Mom, and Dad's bedroom (the largest one), we bought a real nice king-size bed with matching chest of drawer, dresser and two night stands. It was really exciting, at last, moving into a new house and owning our own furniture. I had so much fun decorating and arranging the house. We bought a large kitchen table with six chairs, a sofa, coffee table, two end tables, recliner and matching chair for the sofa. It looked very nice and cozy but not fancy. James was still employed by the freight company in Nashville. They placed him on night shift duty. I was not enthused about having to stay alone at night, but I had Ronnie. I used to get up after his Dad left in the middle of the night, get Ronnie out of his room and put him in bed with me. I felt safer having his presence next to me. Being pregnant added to my insecure and nervous feelings. During the daytime hours, while James slept, I tried to keep things as quiet as I possibly could. When the weather was nice, Ronnie and I played lots outdoors and went for walks around the neighborhood. We even had a small garden planted. He and I used to water it in the evenings and he loved turning the hose on me, and I wound up soaking wet while Ronnie stood there laughing so hard he could hardly catch his breath.

We had lots of problems in our marriage. Dishonesty and mistrust was a big part. I know in my heart that I was too young and lacked maturity when I entered into matrimony, but I kept trying to find ways to make things work out between us. We were two different people with many unlike things in common. I somehow felt that once my parents would be living over here things would get better, and at least I would have someone I could go to and talk to about my problems. We would have an argument or misunderstanding and he would just leave, not telling me where he was going or when he would be back. This only made things worse for me.

Summer was in full bloom and hot. I was getting very big. We had no air conditioning in that house and I had a hard time sleeping nights. We had a window fan that sucked daytime's hot air out during the night and I would sleep better in the early morning hours, but then my almost two year old was ready to start his day, full of action, soon after his Dad arrived from his nightshift. I fixed his breakfast.

Mom and Dad had sold their business and all of their furniture and most other items. They would bring as little as they could get by with, clothes, pictures and personal items. Ronnie's birthday was nearing. He would be two years old on August 7th. I was in big hopes that my parents could be here in time for his birthday celebration. Unfortunately, they did not get here until the 9th, my little brother's birthday. He would have been three years old had he lived. I was now 20 years old and some days felt like 80. I cried and hugged my parents when we picked them up at the airport. I had not seen them in over three years now. I knew I would be happy and content having them live in this country. They, too, seemed to be very happy, especially seeing and getting to hug their grandchild for the very first time. It was a good day. Strangely, Ronnie went right away to my Dad and let him hug him. I told him, that is your "Opa. That is what we call our grandfather in Germany." He could not say "Opa" but he did say "Popa," a name that all of his grandchildren and also great grandchildren used until his death. Ronnie just would have nothing to do with Mom. We told him that was his Mamie. He did say Mamie but would not go to her. He called James' parents "Mamaw and Papaw." He was used to them. I guess my Mom kind of became resentful towards him.

My parents really liked the house and the bedroom furniture we had picked out for them. That made me happy. Dad was concerned about finding a job and getting a car. It was a matter with the language barrier again, but Dad spoke good English at the time. He just did not write it, so I went with him after he bought a used 1954 Ford and asked if the State Trooper would give him an oral test instead of a written one, for he had to have a driver's license in order to get to his job every day. After lots of pleading and arguing, the State Trooper wanted to get rid of me, and he agreed to give Dad an oral test but only if he left me at home the next day. I agreed and let James take him to the driver's license office. Dad passed everything. He also landed his very first job in a tool and dye shop. He had experience and had been licensed in that field.

We were approaching September, and on the night of the 18th I was headed to Springfield Hospital once more where the next morning at 3:05 I gave birth. I did not get the little girl I thought I was going to get but a beautiful blond-haired and blue-eyed baby boy weighing in at six pounds, 13 ounces, just like his older brother but one inch longer. My Mom who also had come to the hospital for my delivery exclaimed, "Oh God gave me back my boy. He is mine." I wanted to say something but I didn't. I somehow felt very sorry for her and her loss. Now that I was a Mother myself I could only imagine the pain that she has had to endure, and I let her think he was her baby as well. After all, she was his grandmother, but let it be known, she preferred him all of her life and spoiled him more than the rest, which caused lots of arguments and hard feelings between us. My Dad used to get on to her as well. He treated all of the boys the same, one like the other, but after I came home from the hospital Mom seemed to take over my job when it came to diapering, bathing or holding little Gary. The only thing she could not do was feed him, for I breast fed him just like I had Ronnie before him. She tried her best to have me bottle feed him, but I stood firm. After a couple of months, Mom found a job in a shoe factory. She rode to work with some friends that picked her up and dropped her back off.

Things were getting very strained between all of us. I decided to find a part-time job. I could work nights where I did not have to worry about the boys. They had family to take care of them, and I would be home with them all day. I went to work in an upper class dinner club. At first I waited on tables. Later, I learned to become a bartender. I made good money and started to save. Mom and Dad wanted to sell the big house and buy a smaller home for the two of them. We needed a place of our own as well. There was just too much interference with my Mom about how to raise our children. It did not work out living together under one roof. I had done it before with his family, but at the time there were no children involved. No two families can live happily under one roof. I knew that I needed to make changes in my own life. Too many things had happened. I had enough money saved and decided to contact an attorney. At that time, I saw no other way out.

I will not go into any details nor will I point a finger at just one person, but I wanted a divorce from my husband. I think that he knew that this was coming. Meanwhile, my parents sold their large house, found a nice two-bedroom brick home a couple of miles away. It, too, sat on a one acre lot and was located in a nice neighborhood. I saw that the house across the street from their just-purchased house had a "for rent" sign in the front yard. I called the phone number on the sign and contacted the owners who lived next door. It was perfect, two bedrooms, living room, kitchen with dining area, and a bathroom. That is all the boys and I would need. My parents lived across the street. They would keep the boys at night when I had to go to work. I moved in, and I can honestly say that for the first time since coming to the U.S. I felt inner peace and happy to live with my two children alone. My attorney told me that my divorce was to be final the second week in July. James had moved in with his parents. Sometimes he stayed at other places.

One morning in early July driving home from work my tires skidded on a wet road. I lost control and hit a brick mailbox at someone's house. I felt a sharp pain on the left side of my head and saw blood dripping down on my white sheath dress, but since I had not hit another vehicle and only someone's mailbox, I thought it would be okay to drive on home and I would contact the owners later when they were up and awake. I arrived at my house and did not feel all that great. My soon to be ex-husband came by the house. He, too, had just gotten off work. He wanted to get the boys and take them to visit their grandparents. When I came to the door he looked at me as if he had just seen a ghost. He said, "What happened to you? You are bleeding from the head." About that moment I felt faint and had to sit down in a nearby chair. He went into the bedroom and got a couple of wet wash cloths. He started wiping the blood off the side of my face. Then, he called my parents and told them that he was taking me to the emergency room at a nearby hospital. He would get back in touch with them later. I did not feel like arguing with him, so I let him drive me. Besides, my head did hurt pretty bad. I was examined and x-rayed, and my diagnosis was a severe concussion and skull fracture at the left side of my head. I was admitted into the hospital with strict orders to lie flat on my back. I had to stay four long days. My parents came constantly and they brought Ronnie and Gary to visit me, which always thrilled me to see my two boys that I was missing so much. Oh, and James came every day also. With each visit he brought a bouquet of flowers, and one evening before leaving he knelt down beside the bed and told me how much he still loved me and the boys as well and would I please give him a chance and not go through with the divorce. I thought about it and agreed to it, another try. After all, I did want the boys to grow up with both of us being there and living in a family environment, something I had to do without for so many years when I was a child. After I got to go home, I called my attorney and told him to call the divorce proceedings off and told him to cancel the divorce proceedings. James moved back in with me and the boys and things seemed to go well for a while.

I kept on working because we wanted to buy our own house as soon as we had enough money saved up. A few months later we heard of a small two-bedroom home that was for sale one street over from my parents' house. The people were older and wanted to move to another state to be near their daughter. They wanted a down payment and then take over the notes on the house. It sounded like a pretty good deal. I had enough money saved up for the down payment. We made arrangements and bought the house. My parent's house and our backyard joined, so my Dad and James took out a part of the fence. That way we could just walk to each other's house without having to walk around the block. Ronnie and Gary thought it was a real neat convenience and after some time there was a trail anyone could spot. I always knew where to look for them if I didn't see them in our backyard.

I need to mention that my Dad and James repaired the people's mailbox that I had hit with my 1949 Buick, and it was one of the bricks that flew in the open window and hit me on the left side of my head.

Things were going pretty good. I quit my job as bartender and started to work part time in a nice department store. I was trained to sell cosmetics and loved doing facials, helping women of all ages choosing a suitable makeup along with eye and lip colors. James also made a change for the better. He was offered to drive on the road which meant lots more money but he would also be gone lots more. Ronnie was now six and Gary four. My parents were a big help to me when he was gone and I had to go work. They did not mind watching the boys. Ronnie loved hanging out with Dad. He got more attention from him than from Mom. All of her attention was focused on Gary, whom I mentioned before, she worshiped the ground he walked on. I had many disagreements with her. Dad would point out to her that it was not right what she did but without any results.

Months passed and I discovered that I was expecting another baby. Once more the news made me very happy. Maybe this time there would be a beautiful little girl that would become a little sister to my very handsome two little boys. I had a very hard time carrying the baby who was situated very low in my abdomen. I had to quit work, quit bowling and numerous other things I could not do if I wanted to carry this baby full term. I had to lie down for one hour each midmorning and midafternoon with my legs elevated. I did everything I was told to do for I wanted this baby so badly. When it was time, the baby came so fast. It was the largest baby I had, 8 pounds, 2 ounces, another beautiful baby boy.

He was born at 7:10 a.m., February 1, 1965. We named him Tony. Snow fell hard all day and into the night. Therefore, we had no visitors because the roads were too dangerous. I did not mind. I would tell the nurse to bring my baby in to be with me. I just lay in bed and watched the snow falling outside, holding this beautiful child in my arms.

I could not wait to get home so that Ronnie and Gary could meet their new baby brother. I never forgot the look on Gary's face when he walked in the house after his Dad had just picked him up from kindergarten. I sat on the couch holding Tony in my arms. Gary looked at me with those beautiful blue eyes and sadly said, "So, I am not the baby anymore?" I almost choked trying to fight back the tears. Then, I reached over with one arm holding him closely. I answered, "You will always be my baby, and I need you and Ronnie to help me to take care of your new little brother." His answer was just plain, "sure." I told him to sit next to me on the sofa and stretch out his legs. Then, I laid Tony in his arms. I did the same with Ronnie when he got home from school. Our little house was pretty full now with the baby that added to our not-so-large bedroom. The boys slept in their room on their bunk beds, but they seemed to be happy and content. James was on the road lots and whenever he came home between trips he had to sleep.

Mom and Dad bought a truck with a camper and started to go on camping trips. They joined a camping group and planned to go on some sort of outing most every week-end. The boys and I would go with them whenever their Dad was gone, which was most weekends. It was good to have some place to go. There were so many great outdoor activities the boys could participate in like swimming, hik-ing, fishing, playing ball and all sorts of outdoor games with other children. We all made lots of new friends and enjoyed spending weekends in their company. There were times when Tony and I stayed home and only Ronnie and Gary would go on camping trips with their grandparents. They always looked forward to getting to go. Dad had also bought a nice boat that added to everyone's pleasure. Sometimes Dad took the two older boys out on the lake to fish. I stayed very busy with three boys now, keeping the house in order, taking them to and from school. Ronnie and Gary both attended a Catholic school so they had to be driven to and from school. I did participate in a three-family car pool transportation. That helped a lot. I only had to drive every third week. Ronnie was now a cub scout and played little league ball. All of that added to more activities. Soon after, Gary did all of that as well. They both took piano lessons. I joined the church's women's club and worked one day a week in the school cafeteria.

James had been a long distance truck driver for several years now. He missed out on lots as far as spending quality time with his wife and children. Once again, our marital relationship became very strained. We seemed to have grown more and more apart. We had hardly anything in common, but we just kept on going and pretending. Then, to both of our surprise, made the unexpected discovery that I was pregnant. It was not planned by no means, and I have to try and be honest and say that I was unhappy the first three months. The way our relationship was going we did not need to have another child, but I carried the baby and loved it as I had all of my previous ones. I had a very difficult birth and went through a very long and hard labor. They could not give me any sedation for any kind. The baby lay in a way that he was born face up, but he was another beautiful baby. He looked a lot like Gary, blond hair and beautiful blue eyes. He weighed 7 pounds, 8 ounces, and we named him John. We now had two brown-eyed and two blue-eyed boys.

Right after I was released from the hospital, James told me that he was being transferred. The company moved all drivers to upstate Virginia. He would look for a place for us to live then the boys and I would be moving as well. The boys nor myself were too excited about this news. We did not want to leave our family and friends, neither did we want to move from the state. James got ready to move. He traded our Rambler station wagon for a new blue-colored Camaro sports car with a black hard top. He left me here in Tennessee for four months driving a 1951 Chevrolet with no air. I had to drive Ronnie to summer school each morning and pick him up at noon. I had a new baby, a three-year-old toddler and an eight and ten year old. I was blessed with having my Mom and Dad here who helped me out lots with the children.

James came home once a month for a long weekend. He still had not found a house for us. Then, at the last of August he said he found a pretty large house for rent. It was just in time for the boys to start their new school. As a matter of fact, we had to stay in a motel until our furniture arrived and the boys had to be taken to school from there for three days until we could finally move into our new residence. It was such a drastic change for us all. The boys and I were so homesick for Tennessee. I cannot write a lot of details of what all happened between us, but after four years in Virginia and 17 ½ years of a struggling marriage, the boys and I moved back. James had promised to move us back as soon as school was out, at the end of May. We had not been living as husband and wife for some time now, and we had known for a long time that the dissolving of our marriage was inevitable. All that was left was our four children. I would never keep him from seeing and being with his children any time he could and just wanted to spend quality time with them. I would never keep them from having a relationship with him. We divorced in July. He went back to Virginia where he had moved into an apartment.

I purchased a house with help from my Dad and got a job in an office. I stayed a single Mom for three years. It was not always easy, but I was used to being alone with the boys since their Dad was gone most of the time anyway. When he was home he had to catch up on his sleep. The only difference now was that I had to go to work, but I did not mind that at all. I liked my job, my boss and my coworkers. We lived in a nice neighborhood and the boys did not have any trouble making new friends. We all seemed to be happy and I felt very peaceful for the first time in years. A nice young man that I had met in Virginia and kept in touch with came to visit us. I started growing very fond of him and he us. After a few visits back and forth, he decided to move here. He got an apartment and found a job in his line of work. We dated for three years. One day he proposed and I accepted. Willie never had any children of his own while he was married to his first wife for several years, so here he was marrying me and four boys whom he loved. I thought this man is crazy for he must really love me a whole lot to take on such responsibility. After all, he was very handsome, he played music and sang, and after we were married he started his own business in construction. He could have had any single young woman but he loved me and I loved him. He became the love of my life and he truly deserves a trophy.

After we were married five years we sold my house and bought a 15-acre place in the outskirts of Nashville. The house was an older house and not as large as the one we moved from, but the countryside around us was beautiful and peaceful. We added several rooms on over the years and covered the outside of the house with vinyl siding. A deck was also added. It was very homey and comfortable. Willie always loved to fool with animals. We had cattle, as many as 22 head at one time, a few horses and even a very mean rooster, and mean he was. He had been so mean. He chased after us and anyone who came into his sight. People that came to visit were afraid to get out of their cars. We decided we had to find him a new home. Ronnie the oldest and Gary had also gotten married and lived in their own homes.

I never got to go see my Aunt Anne Louise. There was never a chance on my side. I was having babies and could not travel that far. She had a job and was also busy with her children and grandchildren. We did have several phone conversations. She later died of cancer. I did get to see Uncle Sal several times. We visited each other a few times. I also met and visited with my cousins and their children and grandchildren. They still live in Massachusetts and in the D.C. and Maryland area. Uncle Sal meanwhile has also passed away and so have both of my parents.

I know that my story is just one of the many people who struggled for survival through a terrible war, but I hope that it makes many people appreciate what a great country they live in. None of us should take anything for granted. Freedom is such a huge thing for anyone to be able to enjoy compared to some other countries and the way some of the people are told how to live, what they can say, do and cannot say. In some countries they would pay with their lives just by admitting that they are Christians.

I have had a very different and sometimes not so happy childhood. I knew at an early age how it felt to say goodbye to my Dad and know he was going to war, maybe to never return. I knew how painful it was to lose everything in one single night and stand homeless with my mother in the midst of a destroyed, bombed and burning city. I have gone so hungry that I cried and so cold that I shivered in a one-room apartment where the windows were covered by ice flowers and crawling into bed under a featherbed to try and get warm. I knew how it felt when other children at school talked about their Dad, the few things they did and how he helped them with their daily homework from school. My Dad spent three and a half years in a French prison camp. I had to make many sacrifices other children never had. Yes, and I struggled through some Rocky years of my first marriage.

Then came the hardest thing that any parent would never want to be faced with – the loss of a child that I, too, had to face. The worst thing when someone tells you your youngest son was killed in an automobile accident. At first, you think there has been a mistake. Then, after being reassured that it is not, for a minute you think that your heart will stop beating. You cannot get any air to breathe. Then you want to fall to your knees and scream out. All the while you hear this voice inside of you telling you over and over. It had to be this way. Yes, this was the biggest mountain I had to overcome. But, I thank God each and every day for my later happy years of my life. I have been happily married for 38 years to my second husband Willie. He is a wonderful man. My three handsome sons are doing very well and are great dads. I have beautiful daughter-in-laws that turned out to be great wives and mothers to our wonderful grandchildren. I have lots of good friends in my life.

At last I can say that I have arrived at my Destination in the U.S.A., the one I always dreamed about. I now live content and happy in this great country. I had become an American citizen five years after I came to the U.S., and I am very proud to call myself an American. God is good and God bless America.

End